# THE CENTRAL MARKET COOKBOOK

# THE CENTRAL MARKET COOKBOOK

*Favorite Recipes from the Standholders of the Nation's Oldest Farmer's Market, Central Market in Lancaster, Pennsylvania*

## Phyllis Pellman Good and Louise Stoltzfus
### Historical Sketches by Stephen Scott

Good Books

Intercourse, Pennsylvania 17534

Design by Cheryl Benner
Photography by Huddle Images

**THE CENTRAL MARKET COOKBOOK**
Copyright © 1989 by Good Books, Intercourse, Pennsylvania 17534
International Standard Book Number: 0-934672-81-4,
hardcover
International Standard Book Number: 0-934672-82-2,
paperback

Library of Congress Card Number: 89-23321

Library of Congress Cataloging-in-Publication Data

Good, Phyllis Pellman, 1948–
    The Central Market cookbook.

    Includes bibliographical references.
    1. Cookery.   I. Stoltzfus, Louise, 1952–
II. Central Market (Lancaster, Pa.)   III. Title.
TX714.G65  1989      641.5      89-23321
ISBN 0-934672-81-4
ISBN 0-934672-82-2 (pbk.)

To all those
who have worked on
Central Market

# Table of Contents

# Introduction

Food is both livelihood and pleasure for the standholders at Lancaster's Central Market.

Perhaps because food is so much a part of these folks' lives, they simply never before thought of writing down recipes of their specialties to share with others.

It was a second-generation standholder who first had the inspiration. The president of the Standholders Association brought enthusiasm to match. With little prompting the standholders began putting on paper the ingredients and procedures for preparing the foods they know so well. In some cases, recipes have been written that were before learned only by watching mothers and grandmothers; other recipes were translated from German to English for the first time. Still others are so familiar and traditional to Lancaster County that standholders weren't sure they merited recording. We encouraged them to offer these recipes, recognizing that many of these foods seem as natural to locals as the meticulous flower beds and covered bridges that draw visitors to the area.

How to organize the gathering of these recipes so that the final collection represented the current flavor of Central Market? We asked standholders to submit three categories of recipes—a food that they sell at their stand or one made with ingredients sold at their stand; a traditional Lancaster County dish that they particularly enjoy; and a personal favorite. In so doing we hoped to capture the regional rootings of the Market, as well as its current more multi-cultural flavor. That spread is here, as it is on Tuesdays, Fridays and Saturdays on Central Market.

This **Cookbook** represents the work of many; first, the standholders who wrote recipes amid tending their truck farms, baking breads and pastries, butchering, curing and making salads. Many of the standholders also tested recipes, along with a group of People's Place Associates. That step brought questions from some of the best cooks—why test recipes when we know they work? It was not their quality or tastiness that we doubted; it was that we wondered if these people, who cook with as little effort as they breathe, would record all the steps needed for the uninitiated!

Viv Hunt and Sam Neff, both from a line of standholder families, gave this whole project a special lift. Norene Lahr, from Lancaster City's Department of Public Works, made many links from the beginning of this book's coming into being. In fact, **Central Market Cookbook** has been a cooperative venture from when Viv first imagined it. Now that it's complete, we invite you to join us in Central Market's tradition of good eating.

—Phyllis Pellman Good and Louise Stoltzfus

# Central Market
# Lancaster, Pennsylvania

Lancaster's Central Market may be an historic site, but it is a vitally active place of commerce and friendship every Tuesday, Friday and Saturday. Then, with dependable regularity, trucks, vans and station wagons crowd the streets and alleys surrounding the Romanesque building. Before daybreak, market standholders "set up"—unpacking and displaying the meat and produce, the breads and pies, the cheeses, spices, flowers, plants, baskets and handmade crafts that draw the market's neighbors, as well as food lovers from far and near. It is a tradition for standholders and market shoppers alike—"Once it's in your blood," they say, "you can't stay away." For what compares with sweet corn pulled just a few hours earlier, with sugar cookies and fudge made only yesterday, with meat cured in nearby smokehouses—and with seeing friends at least once a week?

The market, built in 1889, is old. Older still is the habit of going to market in Lancaster. When Lancaster began as a town in 1730 Andrew and Ann Hamilton deeded property for use as a market place. The 120-foot square lay at the northwest corner of King and Queen Streets adjoining the Centre Square.

George II of England established the market tradition: "And we do further grant for us, our heirs and successors . . . to have, hold and keep . . . two markets in each week." Already in 1744 a visitor in the town remarked, "They have a good market in this town, well filled with provisions of all kinds and prodigiously cheap." A few decades later (in 1776) a British officer paroled in Lancaster remarked, "Food is very plentiful. The markets abound with most excellent cyder and provisions."

The city's interest in the market has protected its integrity and the pristine quality of the food and goods sold there. It was so from the beginning. City Council controlled the affairs of the market. Rent was collected by the city; in 1752 a farmer paid seven shillings and six pence per year. In order to protect the interest of the market the Council ruled that no "chapmen" (itinerant peddlers) were permitted to sell door-to-door in the city or set up stands except at fairs. Effort was also made to establish high standards of quality for the foodstuffs sold at market: there were rules concerning the freshness of meat and that meat not be inflated with air to make it appear more substantial.

The first Lancaster farmers' market was an open-air affair, but by 1757 a market house had been constructed, most likely a rather primitive structure. In 1763 part of the market house was reserved for the storage of three fire engines.

In 1795 Lancaster City Hall was built on the grounds of the market. Adjoining the west end of that building a new market house was constructed in 1798. This was a dual purpose building consisting of brick pillars and arches surrounding an open market place on the first floor and headquarters for a Masonic lodge on the second floor. The Masons shared in the construction cost of the building. The new market officially opened on January 30, 1799. There were 24 stalls, 14 of which were occupied by butchers. The yearly rent was three pounds. This building is still standing, but the first floor has been enclosed and is now occupied by a number of shops.

The relatively small space in the 1798 building was not adequate for long, and an addition was built on the north side of it in 1815. Supplemental market space was also provided by the curb market stands on adjacent streets.

The need to expand the market was considered in 1835 but no property could be purchased at that time. Another unsuccessful attempt was made to buy more space in 1845. Finally, in 1854, several properties were purchased for $32,850. The existing buildings were cleared off and several open-sided pavilions were erected.

The market record books from 1856 to 1875 show four market houses named A, B, C and D, plus the Old Market House. These structures contained from 43 to 53 market stalls each (a total of 180 stalls). An 1875 map shows four long narrow structures in the market area. During most of this same time period, there were also separate fish stands and something called the "Short Market," which included a coffee house, later called a lime house.

These stands were fully enclosed by two large wooden buildings in 1876. Records for this year indicate that Market House Number 1 contained 140 stalls and Market House Number 2 had 120 stalls. Each had six avenues of 12 to 28 stands. The Old Market House with 20 stalls was also still being used, and there were 220 spaces allotted for market stands outside (152 were occupied).

No doubt the city felt considerable pressure to erect a more substantial facility for the Central Market. Four very prominent brick market houses were built in Lancaster by the private sector between 1872 and 1888. Finally, in 1889, an all new, commodious Central Market was erected by the city of Lancaster.

Very little change was made to the Central Market house until 1973. Then, as part of an urban renewal project, the city began major restoration work on the structure. Funding came partly from a $402,000 grant provided by the Department of Housing and Urban Development, available because the market was now listed on the National Register of Historic Places. Matching funds were supplied by the city.

Under the direction of architect S. Dale Kaufman, stands were relocated to provide more aisle space, and a new underground electrical system and sewers were installed. Despite considerable inconvenience to the stand-holders and shoppers, the mayor announced that the market would stay open during the whole renovation process in order to keep a two-century-old tradition alive. The refurbished market house was officially dedicated on March 21, 1975.

Most stalls or units were now six feet long with a few being nine feet or an irregular length. In the new arrangement the stands requiring plumbing facilities for cleanup (fresh meat, fish, etc.) were limited to the rows along three of the walls and rows B and C on the west side.

One long-standing tradition changed in the remodeled market house, with the relocation of the fish stands to the inside of the building. Previously fish was sold only outside at stands along the north side of the market house. Adequate ventilation in the new Central Market took care of a potential odor problem.

A tiny restaurant that occupied the southeast corner of the market was done away with during the remodeling. City Council wished to retain the marketplace character of Central Market, rather than having it become an eating place. However, one sandwich stand was permitted, intended mainly for the convenience of the standholders who wished to eat at the market. Many lunchtime shoppers like to buy a small quantity of meat at one stand and a roll at another stand in order to make their own sandwich while at the market.

There is no doubt that Central Market has become one of Lancaster's main tourist attractions. Despite a deluge of out-of-town visitors, City Council has made a concentrated effort to keep the market a true farmers' market and not one that caters primarily to the tourist trade. The regulations specify that the stands "be used solely for the sale of food products and farm produced goods . . ." Several stands established before the ruling went into effect continued to sell craft and souvenir type items in 1989. No new stands will be granted this privilege.

## Market Days and Hours

An early ordinance established that the market be held on Wednesdays and Saturdays from daybreak to 10:00 a.m. This schedule continued until 1855 when the market began opening on Tuesday and Friday evenings, as well as the regular morning hours. A 1920 ordinance established the hours at 5:00 p.m. to 10:00 p.m. on Tuesdays and Fridays, and until 9:00 a.m. on Wednesdays and Saturdays. No definite opening time was specified for Wednesdays and Saturdays. In the late 1940s the market was again open only two days a week, from 7:30 a.m. to 5:30 p.m. on Tuesdays and Fridays.

When the city of Lancaster closed the Southern Market in 1985, its remaining standholders were offered stands at Central Market. In order to accommodate this influx, Saturday hours were added to the schedule. Currently (in 1989) Central Market is open from 6:00 a.m. to 4:30 p.m. on Tuesdays and Fridays, and from 6:00 a.m. to 2:00 p.m. on Saturdays.

## Market Auctions and Rents

Standholders pay a yearly rent for the stalls they occupy. When a standholder dies or no longer wishes to continue business at the market, the vacant stand goes up for public auction. These auctions usually take place in December. The price paid for a stall at the auction serves as the first year's rent for the stand. In addition to people obtaining a stand for the first time, some market stalls are sold to those already having stands who wish to expand their businesses or move to a better position. Normally, one party is allowed to own no more than four stands at the market.

A market regulation specifies that a vacant stand first be offered for lease "for the same general type of use for which it was used immediately prior to the auction." If no one bids under this provision, then the stand may be open to bidders wishing to use it for other purposes.

When a standholder dies, the market stands may be passed to a spouse or child without being resold at auction. Several market stands are currently occupied by descendants of families who have had stands for three, four and even five generations.

## The Market Master

In the wee hours of every Tuesday, Friday and Saturday morning a lone man's footsteps echo down the brick sidewalks to the Central Market house. He goes to the various entrances, unlocking the large metal doors, just ahead of the trucks bringing fruits, vegetables, meat, fish and baked goods. The man with the keys is the Market Master. It is his responsibility to see that all runs smoothly within the Market.

In the early days the overseer of the market place was called the market clerk. He settled disputes between buyers and sellers and enforced the official rules of the market, including compliance with standard weights and measures. He was to examine all butter and lard and measure all firewood for sale, making allowances for crooked and uneven sticks. The market clerk also oversaw the town fairs.

In 1870 a city ordinance was passed which stated, ". . . The Mayor shall appoint a Market Master, whose duty it shall be to attend the market during market hours, and such other times as shall be necessary . . .; he shall prevent the sale of or exposing to sale all unsound and unwholesome provisions . . ." The responsibility of keeping the market clean and the removal of snow were also given to the Market Master.

That Central Market has retained its vitality for more than 250 years is due to a cooperative effort between the city and the standholders. The city has protected the Market; the standholders have demonstrated resiliency by providing the traditional along with the novel. It is that mix of old favorites and the experimental that characterizes Central Market—Chow Chow residing comfortably near Tarragon Chicken Pasta, Sticky Buns sharing the aisle with Brioches, Cup Cheese sitting only stands away from Brie.

The Market belongs to and reflects the Lancaster community. The quality that is Central Market is expressed not only in the magnificent building which houses it, but also in the food and wares that are sold there—much of it home-grown and home-prepared from Lancaster's truck farms, home bakeries and butcher shops. May it continue as it was designated in the City of Lancaster's charter: "to have, hold and keep . . . market . . . in every week of the year forever"!

# APPETIZERS
## AND
# BEVERAGES

# Cabbage Centerpiece for Appetizer

Head of cabbage
Cherry tomatoes
Olives
Radishes
Mushrooms

Pickles
Pepper strips
Baby carrots
Broccoli flowerets
Cauliflower flowerets

1. Trim bottom of cabbage head so it will sit level on a plate.
2. Put assortment of vegetables on round toothpicks.
3. Arrange vegetables on cabbage by pushing toothpicks into the cabbage head.
4. After party, use cabbage for slaw.

*—Doris Shenk, Donegal Gardens*

# Broiled Cheesy Appetizers

*Makes 20 servings*

1 cup medium cheddar cheese, shredded
⅓ cup bacon bits
¼ cup mayonnaise
2 Tbsp. onion, chopped
20 slices round party rye bread

1. Mix all ingredients except bread.
2. Spread about 1 Tbsp. mixture on each slice of bread.
3. Set broiler at 550°.
4. Place broiler tray at least 4 inches from heat.
5. Broil 1–2 minutes or until cheese melts.

Our family traditionally serves these on Christmas Eve.

*—Frances Kiefer, Kiefer's Meat and Cheese*

# Baked Cheese-Filled Pastry

*Makes 15 rolls*

½ lb. feta cheese, crumbled, or mozzarella cheese, shredded
¼ cup flat-leaf parsley, finely chopped
8–10 Tbsp. margarine or butter, melted
15 sheets phyllo pastry, ready-made

1. Mix cheese and parsley together.
2. Using pastry brush, brush melted butter on one side of a sheet of pastry. Fold sheet in half to make a long rectangle. Brush the outside edges with butter.
3. Place 1 Tbsp. of cheese mixture on one short-sided end of pastry.

4. Fold long edges toward the center about ½ inch on each side.
5. Starting at the short end with cheese mixture, roll pastry up into a tight cylinder. Repeat process with each piece of phyllo pastry.
6. Place rolls into greased 7″ × 10″ baking pan with seam side down.
7. Bake at 350° for 25–30 minutes or until golden brown.

*—Dorothy Koth, Habibi's*

# Cheese Ball

**8-oz. pkg. cream cheese, softened**
**1 cup mozzarella cheese, grated and softened**
**1 pkg. George Washington's® seasoning and broth mix**
**¼ cup pecans, finely chopped**

1. Mix cream cheese, mozzarella cheese and Washington's® seasoning in small bowl until well blended. Shape into a round ball.
2. Flatten slightly and roll ball in pecans.
3. Refrigerate overnight and serve with variety of crackers.

*—Joyce Deiter, Eisenberger's Baked Goods*

**Variation:**
Substitute your own favorite soup mix for George Washington's® seasoning and broth mix.

# Crabbies

*Makes 12 main servings or 48 appetizer servings*

**¼ lb. butter**
**2 cups prepared cheese spread**
**1½ Tbsp. mayonnaise**
**½ tsp. garlic salt**
**7-oz. can crab meat or ½ lb. fresh or frozen crab**
**6 English muffins, split**

1. Soften butter and cheese to room temperature.
2. Mix butter, cheese, mayonnaise, salt and crab meat.
3. Spread on split muffins, place on cookie sheet and freeze.
4. When frozen remove from cookie sheet and store in plastic bag.
5. When ready to serve do not thaw.
6. Place frozen crabbies on cookie sheet and broil until bubbly and crisp.

*—Judy Weidman, customer of John R. Stoner*

**Variation:**
Quarter each muffin half and serve as an appetizer.

◆

# Shrimp Jello Spread

*Makes 3 cups spread*

3-oz. pkg. lemon gelatin
1 cup boiling water
1 cup chili sauce
¼ cup horseradish
1 tsp. lemon juice
5-oz. can small shrimp, rinsed and drained

1. Add gelatin to boiling water.
2. When slightly thickened, add all other ingredients.
3. Chill several hours in small mold until firm.
4. Unmold on serving dish and serve with crackers.

—*Ethel Stoner, John R. Stoner Vegetables*

# Shrimp Cheese Spread

*Makes 1 pint*

½ lb. sharp cheese, grated
1 can shrimp pieces, chopped
1 small onion, finely grated
1 tsp. celery salt
1 cup mayonnaise
1 Tbsp. Worchestershire® sauce

1. Mix all ingredients and refrigerate.
2. Serve with an assortment of crackers.

—*Ethel Stoner, John R. Stoner Vegetables*

I started working for S. Clyde Weaver when I was 28 years old. I have been on Central Market for 37 years. The best part of the job is meeting people. I remember people by what they buy. For example, I remembered a man who now lives in Detroit because he always came in to buy our old-fashioned ham.

—*Ben E. Greenawalt, S. Clyde Weaver, Inc.*

# Spinach Squares

*Makes 10 – 12 servings*

| | |
|---|---|
| 1 cup flour | 6 Tbsp. butter, softened |
| 1 tsp. salt | 2 cups fresh spinach or |
| 1 tsp. baking powder | 1 pkg. frozen spinach |
| 2 eggs, beaten | 1 lb. sharp cheddar cheese, |
| 1 cup milk | grated |
| | 1 onion, chopped |

1. Sift flour, salt and baking powder into a large bowl. Add eggs, milk and butter and mix well.
2. If using fresh spinach cook, drain and chop. If using frozen spinach thaw and drain.
3. Add spinach, cheese and onion to flour and egg mixture. Spread into a greased 9″ × 13″ pan.
4. Bake at 350° for 30 minutes. Cool 10 – 15 minutes or long enough to cut into squares. Serve warm.

This recipe disappears like magic at a party. This will become a tradition in our family.

*— Ethel Stoner, John R. Stoner Vegetables*

# Spinach Crab Cakes

*Makes 12 – 15 servings*

| | |
|---|---|
| 1¼ lbs. fresh spinach | ½ cup Parmesan cheese |
| ¾ cup margarine | 1 Tbsp. garlic salt |
| 2 large onions, chopped | 1 scant Tbsp. pepper |
| 6 eggs, beaten | 1 lb. claw crabmeat |
| ½ tsp. thyme | 2 cups herb bread filling |

1. Cook and drain the spinach.
2. Melt margarine. Add all other ingredients except herb filling and mix well.
3. Add 1 cup herb filling and mix well.
4. Form mixture into small patties.
5. Grind 1 cup herb filling. Bread spinach patties with ground herb filling.
6. Deep fry or freeze for future use.

Delicious! May be served as main dish, as a sandwich or as an appetizer.

*— Doris Shenk, Donegal Gardens*

# Crescent-Veggie Bar

*Makes 10–12 servings*

2 pkgs. crescent rolls
raw vegetables (broccoli, cauliflower, peppers, etc.)
2 8-oz. pkgs. cream cheese
1 pkg. ranch dressing mix
¾ cup mayonnaise
½–1 lb. cheese, grated

1. Pat crescent roll dough in a flat layer in 9″ × 13″ pan.
2. Bake at 425° until brown, about 8–10 minutes. Cool.
3. Beat cream cheese, dressing mix and mayonnaise together until smooth and spread over baked crescent roll dough.
4. Chop vegetables finely and spread evenly over dough.
5. Cover with grated cheese, cut into squares and serve.

*— Ethel Stoner, John R. Stoner Vegetables*

# Egg Rolls

*Makes 24 servings*

3 Tbsp. cooking oil
½ lb. ground pork
½ lb. shrimp, shelled and
   deveined
¼ cup water chestnuts,
   minced
1 lb. carrots, chopped
1 lb. cabbage, chopped

½ cup onion, chopped
1 Tbsp. soy sauce
1 Tbsp. salt
1 Tbsp. black pepper
1 egg, beaten
24 egg roll wraps
oil for deep frying

1. Heat 1 Tbsp. oil in frying pan and stir fry pork about 5 minutes. Set aside.
2. Heat 2 Tbsp. oil in pan and add shrimp, water chestnuts, carrots, cabbage and onion. Cook, stirring constantly, until shrimp turns pink. Add seasonings and cooked pork. Stir until all ingredients are well mixed.
3. Spoon ingredients onto egg roll wraps. Wrap ingredients in shells and brush edges with beaten eggs to hold them together.
4. Bring oil for deep frying to 300°. Deep fry egg rolls for 7 minutes or until golden brown. Drain off excess oil before serving.

*— Tuyen Kim Ho, Kim's Candies*

# Spiced Nuts

2 Tbsp. cold water
1 egg white
½ cup sugar
½ tsp. salt

¼ tsp. cinnamon
¼ tsp. ground cloves
¼ tsp. ground allspice
¾ – 1 lb. pecan or walnut
halves

1. Add water to the egg white and beat lightly with a fork.
2. Add all dry ingredients and mix well.
3. Add nuts to the mixture and coat them. Place nuts flat side down on a greased cookie sheet.
4. Bake 1 hour at 250° until brown. Cool and store in a tin.

My wife's great aunt from Hagerstown always serves these with her Christmas cookies.

— *Sam Neff, S. Clyde Weaver, Inc.*

# Smores

*Makes 48 squares*

⅔ cup light corn syrup
2 Tbsp. butter
2 cups semi-sweet chocolate
chips

1 tsp. vanilla
10-oz. pkg. Golden Graham®
cereal
3 cups mini marshmallows

1. Heat syrup, butter and chocolate chips just to boiling in 3-quart saucepan, stirring constantly. Remove from heat and stir in vanilla.
2. In a large bowl pour mixture over cereal. Toss quickly until cereal is completely covered with chocolate.
3. Fold in marshmallows, 1 cup at a time.
4. Press mixture evenly into well-greased 9″ × 13″ pan. Let stand until firm (about 1 hour).
5. Cut into 1½-inch squares. Store in cool place.

Great snack or finger food!

— *Joyce Deiter, Eisenberger's Baked Goods*

◆

# Orange Julius Beverage

*Makes 4 servings*

½ cup frozen orange juice concentrate
¾ cup water
¾ cup milk
⅓ cup sugar
¾ tsp. vanilla
9 ice cubes, broken

Blend all ingredients in blender and serve.

Delicious and refreshing summertime drink!
—*Joyce Deiter, Eisenberger's Baked Goods*

# Milk Punch

*Makes 24 8-oz. servings*

½ gallon milk
½ gallon orange juice
1 pint orange sherbet
½ gallon orange drink
16-oz. can ginger ale

Mix all ingredients and serve.
—*Mildred Brackbill, Utz's Potato Chips*

# Cranberry Frappé

*Makes 25 servings or 5 quarts*

12-oz. can frozen cranberry or red raspberry juice
46-oz. can unsweetened chilled pineapple juice
1 cup sugar
½ gallon red raspberry sherbet
1 quart lemon-lime chilled carbonated beverage or 1 quart
  raspberry sparkler

1. Mix cranberry juice with water as directed on can.
2. Add pineapple juice and sugar. Mix well.
3. Cut sherbet into pieces and place in punch bowl.
4. Add juice mixture and mix well. Immediately before serving
pour in carbonated beverage and stir well.
—*Ethel Stoner, John R. Stoner Vegetables*

# Cranberry Punch

*Makes 23 8-oz. servings*

9 cups cranberry juice
9 cups unsweetened pineapple juice
4½ cups water
1 cup brown sugar
4½ tsp. whole cloves
4 broken cinnamon sticks
¼ tsp. salt

1. Mix cranberry and pineapple juices with water and brown sugar.
2. Pour into 30-cup percolator.
3. Place cloves and spices into the filter.
4. Turn on percolator and serve hot when it is finished.

*— Viv Hunt, Viv's Varieties*

# Tropical Fruit Punch

*Makes 25 8-oz. servings*

5 bananas, well ripened
46-oz. can pineapple juice
16-oz. can frozen orange juice
46 oz. water
4 tsp. lemon juice
1 2-liter bottle ginger ale

1. Blend bananas and half of pineapple juice in blender.
2. Mix with all other ingredients except ginger ale.
3. Immediately before serving add ginger ale and crushed ice.

**Hints:**
Mix ahead of time and freeze.
Use unsweetened juices and diet soda for a diet punch.
Excellent for bridal showers, parties, and picnics.

*— Esther Sangrey, Martin's Home Baked Goods*

◆

# Party Punch

*Makes 1 gallon*

**1 lemon**
**2 limes**
**2 9-oz. cans frozen orange juice, thawed**
**3 cups pineapple juice**
**6 cups cold water**
**42 ozs. ginger ale, chilled**

1. Squeeze the juice from the lemon and limes and strain into punch bowl.
2. Add orange juice, pineapple juice and water. Chill.
3. Before serving add ginger ale.

Garnish with frozen lime, lemon or orange slices.

— *Mary Ellen Campbell, Baskets of Central Market*

# Banana Slushy Punch

*Makes 25 servings*

| | |
|---|---|
| **46 oz. water** | **6 oz. orange juice concentrate** |
| **3 cups sugar** | |
| **5 medium, ripe bananas** | **4 Tbsp. lemon juice** |
| **46-oz. can pineapple juice** | **6 quarts ginger ale** |

1. Combine water and sugar, bring to a boil and stir until dissolved. Boil gently for 3 minutes (uncovered). Cool.
2. Combine bananas and half of pineapple juice in blender.
3. Add sugar syrup and remaining pineapple juice to banana mixture.
4. Add orange and lemon juice and mix thoroughly.
5. Divide mixture into 3 containers and freeze.
6. Before serving, thaw mixture (approximately 1 hr.) to a very thick chunky consistency.
7. When ready to serve, slowly add 2 quarts ginger ale to each container of mixture. Stir until mixture is a slushy, pourable consistency.

Garnish each cup with a floating orange slice or half a strawberry. Very refreshing for hot summer days.

— *Scott Summy, Willow Valley Farms*

# Citrus Punch

*Makes 12–18 servings*

1 can frozen orange juice
1 can frozen lemonade
1 can frozen limeade
1 quart water
1 quart ginger ale

1. Mix all ingredients except ginger ale.
2. When ready to serve stir in ginger ale. Float orange and/or lemon slices on top.

Great summertime punch!

*— Ruth Eshelman, Givant's*

# Rhubarb Punch

*Makes 3–4 quarts*

1 quart one-inch slices rhubarb
2 cups sugar
6 lemons
1½ cups pineapple juice
1 quart ginger ale

1. Cover rhubarb pieces with water and cook about 10 minutes until soft. Drain. Makes about 3 cups juice.
2. Dissolve sugar in 2 cups water and cook about 10 minutes.
3. To sugar syrup add juice of lemons and pineapple juice.
4. Mix well and add rhubarb juice. Mix again.
5. When ready to serve, add ginger ale and ice cubes.

Surprisingly delightful taste!

*— Ruth Eshleman, Givant's Bakery*

◆

# Concord Grape Juice

**8 lbs. Concord grapes**
**4 quarts water**
**¾ lb. granulated sugar**

1. Weigh grapes after removing stems.
2. Wash grapes and cover with water in a kettle. Let boil until shells and grapes are separated.
3. Pour mixture first through a coarse and then through a fine sieve. Repeat process several times.
4. Add sugar to strained juice and boil for 5 minutes.
5. Put in jars while juice is hot and let seal.

We sell New York state Concord grapes at our stand in the fall of the year. I serve this with ginger ale after our Christmas meal.
—*Ruth Widders, Irwin S. Widders Produce*

**Variations:**
1. Pour mixture through a fine sieve before serving, if desired.
2. Add more water, sugar or ginger ale before serving.

# Lemonade

*Makes 3 quarts*

**6 lemons**
**1½ cups sugar**
**2½ cups water**

1. Slice lemons into rings or thin slices and seed.
2. Place lemon slices into a large bowl or kettle. Add sugar and pound with a wooden mallet to extract the juice.
3. Let stand for one-half hour. Add cold water and ice cubes.
4. Stir well and serve.

Using the rind, pulp and juice gives this an excellent flavor and healthfully quenches thirst.
—*Ruth Widders, Irwin S. Widders Produce*

# BREADS

◆

# Homemade Bread

*Makes 4 loaves*

½ tsp. sugar
½ pkg. yeast
½ cup lukewarm water
3 cups lukewarm water

1½ level Tbsp. salt
¼ cup vegetable oil
½ cup sugar
2½ quarts bread flour

1. Add sugar and yeast to ½ cup lukewarm water. Let stand for 5 minutes.
2. Add 3 cups lukewarm water, salt, oil, sugar and 1 quart flour and beat until thoroughly mixed. Work in 1½ quarts flour and knead for 10 minutes. Let rise until double.
3. Knead 2–3 minutes and let stand for about an hour. Knead again for 1–2 minutes and put into greased bread pans. Let rise again.
4. Bake at 350° for 30 minutes.
5. Cool slightly. Put into plastic bags while still warm.

— *Mary Ellen Speicher, Sallie Y. Lapp*

# Oatmeal Bread

*Makes 2 large loaves or 2 dozen rolls*

½ cup brown sugar
1 tsp. salt
1 cup quick oats
½ cup whole wheat flour
2 Tbsp. margarine, melted

2 cups boiling water
1 Tbsp. yeast
½ cup warm water
4–5 cups white flour

1. Combine brown sugar, salt, oats, whole wheat flour and margarine in a large mixing bowl.
2. Pour boiling water over mixture and mix well.
3. Dissolve yeast in warm water. When batter has cooled to lukewarm, stir in yeast mixture. Add white flour.
4. Knead on board for 10 minutes. Place in greased bowl, cover and let rise until doubled.
5. Punch down and let rise again.
6. Punch down again and shape into 2 loaves or 24 small rolls.
7. Bake at 350° for 30–40 minutes.

The oatmeal, whole wheat flour and brown sugar make this bread unusually tasty.

— *Ruth Widders, Irwin S. Widders Produce*

# Date-Nut Loaf

*Makes 10 – 12 servings*

| | |
|---|---|
| 1 cup all-purpose flour | 1 lb. English walnuts |
| ½ tsp. salt | ¾ cup sugar |
| 2 tsp. baking powder | 4 eggs, separated |
| 1 lb. dates, chopped | 1 tsp. vanilla |

1. Sift flour. Measure and add salt and baking powder. Sift again. Add chopped dates and whole kernels of walnuts.
2. Add sugar to mixture and stir until well blended. Add well-beaten egg yolks to mixture and beat until thoroughly mixed. Fold in stiffly beaten egg whites and vanilla.
3. Pour into a well-greased loaf pan or rectangular cake pan.
4. Bake at 300° for 1½ hours if using loaf pan. Bake at 275 – 300° for 1 to 1½ hours if using rectangular pan.

I remember this recipe from childhood. Mother would have it at Christmas instead of fruitcake.

*— Ruth Martin, C. Z. Martin Sons*

# Lemon Bread

*Makes 1 loaf*

| | |
|---|---|
| 1 cup sugar | ½ tsp. salt |
| 5 Tbsp. butter, softened | 1½ cups flour |
| 2 eggs | 1 tsp. baking powder |
| ½ cup milk | ½ cup walnuts, chopped |
| grated rind of 1 lemon | (optional) |

*Glaze Ingredients:*
juice of 1 lemon
½ cup sugar

1. Cream together sugar and butter. Blend in eggs, milk and lemon rind.
2. Mix together remaining ingredients. Add to creamed mixture, blending well.
3. Pour into greased 4″ × 8″ pan. Bake 1 hour at 350°.
4. Cool 5 minutes, then remove from pan.
5. Spoon glaze over *warm* bread.

*— Mary Ellen Campbell, Baskets of Central Market*

◆

# Honey Banana Bread

*Makes 1 loaf*

½ cup shortening  
¼ cup sugar  
½ tsp. salt  
½ cup honey  
1 tsp. baking soda

3 large bananas, mashed  
2 eggs, beaten  
2 cups flour  
1 tsp. vanilla  
¼ cup nuts, chopped

1. Blend shortening, sugar and salt. Add all other ingredients and mix well.
2. Pour into a well-greased loaf pan and bake at 350° for 60–70 minutes.

*—Elva E. Martin, Rudolph Breighner*


# Aunt Beth's Potato Buns

*Makes 40 small rolls*

1 cup mashed potatoes  
½ cup potato water  
2 eggs  
⅓ cup sugar  
½ tsp. salt

1 pkg. yeast  
½ cup flour  
½ cup lard  
⅓ cup sugar  
additional flour to make soft dough

1. At 5 p.m. mix mashed potatoes, ½ cup water used to boil potatoes, eggs, ⅓ cup sugar, salt, yeast and ½ cup flour. Let stand.
2. At 10 p.m. add ½ cup lard, ⅓ cup sugar and enough flour to make a soft dough. Knead slightly to create a soft dough. Let rise until the next morning.
3. At 7 a.m. punch down the dough and form into whatever size rolls you prefer. Put on baking sheets. Let rise until 10 a.m.
4. Bake at 350° until slightly brown, about 15 minutes.

**Hint:** Keep dough and ingredients at room temperature at all times. Also keep out of all drafts. These rolls are light and very good.

*—Edith R. Weaver, Frank Weaver Greenhouses*

# Dinner Rolls

*Makes 3 dozen rolls*

| | |
|---|---|
| 1 cup milk | 3 eggs |
| ½ cup butter | 4½ – 5 cups flour |
| ½ cup sugar | pinch salt |
| 1 pkg. yeast | |

1. Scald milk. Remove from heat. Stir in butter and sugar. Cool to 85°, add yeast and wait until dissolved.
2. Stir eggs into milk, then mix in flour and salt. Stop when dough is soft, not sticky or too dry. Let rise until double (about 45 minutes).
3. Divide into 3 balls, roll out each into a circle, then cut each into 12 pieces like a pizza.
4. Roll each slice up from the outside toward the center and place on *lightly* greased baking sheet.
5. Let rise until doubled (about 30 minutes) and bake at 350° for 10 – 15 minutes until browned.

*— Peter Kovalec, Windows on Steinman Park*

# Crescent Nut Rolls

*Makes 3 dozen rolls*

| *Dough Ingredients:* | *Filling Ingredients:* |
|---|---|
| 2 cups flour | ¾ cup pecans, chopped fine |
| 1 cup butter, softened | ¾ cup granulated sugar |
| ¾ cup sour cream | 1 tsp. cinnamon |
| 1 egg yolk | |

1. Mix dough ingredients like pie dough and form into 6 balls.
2. Wrap each ball in plastic wrap and refrigerate overnight.
3. Roll and cut into crescent strips. (Roll dough like pie dough, then use pastry wheel to cut the circle in half, then each half in thirds.) Each ball will make 6 crescents.
4. Mix all filling ingredients and spread over each crescent shape. Roll up, starting at wide end, ending with the narrow end.
5. Place on greased cooking sheet and bake at 375° for 12 minutes or until golden brown. Be careful not to let the bottoms get too dark.
6. When cool dust with confectioner's sugar, using a small strainer and shaking it.

**Hint:** All balls may be rolled and prepared before starting to bake.

These cookies may be frozen. They are a family favorite at Christmastime.

*— Joyce Deiter, Eisenberger's Baked Goods*

# The
# Market Boys
## and their
# Wagons

Shoppers leaving the farmers' markets with full baskets often found their burdens too great to bear. Enterprising boys and a few girls waited with their express wagons (or sometimes sleds in winter) around the market houses to offer their assistance. Few of these youngsters were over 12 years old.

Many market-goers had favorite wagon boys whom they patronized regularly. Some people reserved a boy and his wagon when going into the market. If the boy was still waiting when the person was finished shopping, an extra tip was in order. Elderly shoppers often asked boys to carry their baskets through the market as they shopped. Those who could not be early birds but still wanted to get the proverbial worm made arrangements with boys to go to the market as early as possible and have the cream of the crop set aside until they arrived.

In the 1920s the fee for transporting a basket ranged from 10¢ to 25¢, depending on the length of the trip. For carrying a basket around as a person shopped, a youngster was paid 10¢. A boy might make as many as a dozen trips in a day. The distance could range from a short walk to the trolley or bus stop, to going more than a mile. A few boys specialized in long-distance traveling and equipped their bicycles to carry baskets. Some shoppers did not accompany the delivery boy home but arranged to have their market baskets deposited on back-door steps while they did additional shopping. Boys could also earn extra money helping standholders to unload and load their wares.

Of course, it was in the summertime, on Saturday mornings and during evening market hours that the school boys had their greatest opportunity to earn money. Some of the more energetic youth managed to get in a few trips early in the mornings and during lunch breaks throughout the school year. Truant officers kept a special lookout for industrious hooky-players at the market houses. A speedy youth could earn a decent day's wages, but he needed to be steady and agile. Being in too much of a hurry often meant an upset wagon, with apples, oranges and potatoes rolling down the street.

# Sticky Buns

*Makes 12 servings*

**Dough Ingredients:**
1 pkg. dry yeast
⅛ cup warm water
1 cup scalded milk
¼ cup granulated sugar
1 tsp. salt
1½ Tbsp. shortening
2 eggs
2 – 3 cups flour
¼ cup butter, melted
½ cup brown sugar
2 Tbsp. cinnamon

**Topping Ingredients:**
½ cup brown sugar
⅛ cup margarine
1 Tbsp. corn syrup
⅛ cup water

1. Soak yeast in warm water. Meanwhile, scald milk and add sugar, salt and shortening. Cool mixture until lukewarm. Add yeast and eggs to the milk mixture.
2. Add 2 cups flour. Add more flour to make a soft dough. Knead mixture until smooth and elastic. Let rise 45 minutes.
3. Roll out dough into a rectangular shape. Spread melted butter, brown sugar and cinnamon over the dough. Roll up dough and cut into ¾-1 inch pieces.
4. Mix all topping ingredients and heat until sugar is well dissolved. Pour topping into two greased 8″ cake pans. Place sticky buns onto the topping and let rise for 1 hour.
5. Bake at 375° for 15 – 20 minutes.

Excellent sliced in half and grilled for breakfast.
— *Thomas Martin, Willow Valley Farms*

**Variation:**
Add nuts, raisins or coconut.

**Central Market is a unique marketplace. Thanks to the city of Lancaster and Mayor Art Morris the renovation of the market preserved the original building which was the leading edge in architectural styles when it was built in 1889. Visitors often comment about the beauty and character of the building.**
— *Paul L. Neff, S. Clyde Weaver, Inc.*

# Quick Sticky Buns

*Makes 24 servings*

*Dough Ingredients:*
1½ cups flour
2 pkgs. dry yeast
¾ cup milk
½ cup water
¼ cup butter
¼ cup sugar
1 tsp. salt
1 egg
1¾ cups flour

*Topping Ingredients:*
¾ cup butter
1 cup brown sugar
1 tsp. cinnamon
1 cup nuts, chopped
1 Tbsp. corn syrup
1 Tbsp. water

1. In a large mixing bowl combine 1½ cups flour and yeast.
2. In a saucepan heat milk, water, butter, sugar and salt until warm. Do not bring to a boil. Pour this mixture over yeast and flour. Add egg and beat on high speed for 3 minutes.
3. By hand stir in 1¾ cups flour. Cover and let rise for 30 minutes.
4. While dough is rising combine all topping ingredients in a saucepan and heat until melted. Pour topping into a greased 9″ × 13″ pan.
5. Knead dough several minutes. Drop by tablespoonfuls onto the topping. Bake at 375° for 15–18 minutes. Cool for 1 minute.
6. Cover pan with a cookie sheet and carefully invert contents of pan onto cookie sheet.

Note: You can let dough rise in an oven turned to warm setting.
— *Janice Kreider, Eisenberger's Baked Goods*

# Pfannebecker's Dewey Buns

*Makes 6 dozen*

2 lbs. flour
4 ozs. sugar
4 ozs. shortening
½ oz. salt

1 pint water
2 ozs. compressed yeast
1 oz. malt (optional)
2–3 cups confectioner's sugar

1. Mix flour, sugar, shortening and salt gently to distribute salt. Add water, yeast and malt. Mix well.
2. Place on work surface and mold. Knead well into a round ball.
3. Place in greased bowl and cover with cloth. Let rise until double in size (about 30–45 minutes).
4. Divide dough into pieces and roll into long strips. Cut strips into one-ounce pieces and roll again into 5-inch long strips. Place strips on floured cloth or pan.

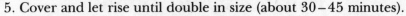

5. Cover and let rise until double in size (about 30–45 minutes).
6. Fry in deep fat at 375° until brown.
7. Cool and sugar by placing in plastic bag with confectioner's sugar. Shake bag and remove buns.

*— William L. Pfannebecker and Lydia Smith*

The Pfannebecker Stand on Central Market was well-known in the local community for its Dewey Buns. Although the stand is no longer on the market, the cookbook did not seem complete without the Dewey Bun recipe. Our sincere appreciation to the Pfannebecker family for sharing this recipe with the *Central Market Cookbook.*

# Blueberry Oat Muffins

*Makes 1 dozen muffins*

| | |
|---|---|
| 1 cup uncooked rolled oats | ¾ cup brown sugar, lightly packed |
| 1 cup schmierkase or butter-milk | ¼ cup corn oil or margarine |
| 1 cup flour | 1 egg, beaten |
| 1 tsp. baking powder | 1 cup fresh or frozen blue-berries |
| ½ tsp. baking soda | |
| ½ tsp. salt | |

1. Combine oats and schmierkase in a small bowl. Let stand.
2. In another bowl combine flour, baking powder, soda, salt and brown sugar. Stir and blend well.
3. Add oil or melted margarine and egg to the oat mixture. Mix well. Add dry ingredients to oat mixture and stir until ingredients are moistened. Gently fold in blueberries.
4. Fill well-greased muffin tins ¾ full. Bake at 400° for 15–20 minutes.

Make these ahead of time and freeze them. Take out of freezer and heat in microwave before serving.
*— Mary Catherine Bowman, Shenk's Cheese Co.*

**Variation:**
Substitute chopped apples plus 1 tsp. cinnamon for blueberries.

# Banana Raisin Muffins

*Makes 1 dozen muffins*

1 cup all-purpose flour
1 cup oatmeal
1 Tbsp. baking powder
½ tsp. cinnamon
1 cup skim milk
½ cup ripe bananas, mashed

½ cup raisins (optional)
¼ cup vegetable oil
¼ cup brown sugar, firmly
  packed
1 egg white

1. Combine flour, oats, baking powder and cinnamon. Set aside.
2. Combine remaining ingredients, then add to dry ingredients mixing just until dry ingredients are moistened.
3. Line 12 medium muffin cups with paper baking cups or oil the muffin tins themselves and fill ¾ full.
4. Bake at 375° for 25 minutes.

These make a quick, easy breakfast food and are a good way to use up ripe bnanas.

— *Rose Meck, Robert S. Meck*

# Fassnachts

*Makes 50 fassnachts*

¼ cup warm water
1 pkg. yeast
2 Tbsp. sugar
2½ cups lukewarm milk
4½ cups flour

4 eggs, beaten
½ cup lard, melted
1 cup sugar
dash of salt
5½ cups flour

1. Dissolve yeast in warm water.
2. Mix next three ingredients together, then add to yeast mixture. Set in warm place and let rise overnight.
3. In the morning add next four ingredients. Add last batch of flour slowly; it may not all be needed. Dough should be sticky but able to be handled.
4. Let rise until doubled, approximately 2 hours.
5. Roll out and cut with biscuit or doughnut cutter, with or without a center hole. Let rise 1 hour.
6. Deep fry in hot oil at 375° for several minutes, turning until brown on both sides.

This is not only a family favorite, but also rekindles fond memories of days spent with my friend Ruth Eshelman from whom I learned the tricks of this delicious treat!

— *Hilda Funk, Givant's*

Among the Pennsylvania Germans, Shrove Tuesday is known as Fassnacht Day (night before the fast). In a symbolic effort to rid their homes of leavening agents and to feast before Lent, many Pennsylvania German cooks spend part of this day making Fassnachts. The cakes are made of a yeast dough, and tradition requires that they be shaped in squares or rectangles with slits cut in them.

# Mashed Potato Doughnuts

*Makes 8 dozen doughnuts*

*Doughnut Ingredients:*
1 cup butter or margarine,
    softened
1 cup sugar
2 cups mashed potatoes
1 quart scalded whole milk
3 pkgs. yeast
¾ cup lukewarm water
4 cups flour
2 eggs
1 Tbsp. salt
10–11 more cups flour

*Glaze Ingredients:*
1 lb. confectioner's sugar
½ cup rich milk
2 Tbsp. butter, melted
1 tsp. vanilla
¼ tsp. mace (optional)

1. Mix butter or margarine, sugar and mashed potatoes while potatoes are still hot.
2. Add scalded milk to potato mixture. Put yeast into lukewarm water and proof. Add to potato mixture. Add 4 cups flour and beat mixture. Let stand for 20 minutes.
3. Add eggs and salt. Mix in additional flour until mixture becomes satiny. Let rise for 2 hours.
4. Shape dough into doughnuts and let rise about 20 minutes.
5. Deep fry in hot oil at 375–400°. Glaze while doughnuts are still hot.
6. To prepare glaze mix sugar and rich milk. Add melted butter and vanilla. Add mace, if desired. Dip hot doughnuts into glaze.

Hint: I prefer a fine-grained flour.
                    —*Joanne Warfel, S. Clyde Weaver, Inc.*

# Turkey Vegetable Soup

*Makes 8 – 10 servings*

1 lb. ground turkey
1 cup onion, chopped
salt and pepper to taste
½ tsp. garlic powder
1 cup potatoes, diced
1 cup carrots, grated
1 cup green beans, chopped
1 cup fresh corn

1 cup fresh baby limas
3 cups water
2 tsp. salt
1 tsp. basil
1 bay leaf
4 cups tomatoes, peeled and
   chopped
1 cup peas

1. Cook ground turkey and onion together until meat is lightly browned. Season with salt, pepper and garlic powder. Drain off excess fat.
2. In large 6-quart kettle combine all vegetables except peas and tomatoes. Add water. Bring to a boil and cook for 10 – 15 minutes.
3. Add meat, seasonings and tomatoes. Cover and simmer for 1 hour. Add peas for the last 10 minutes.

I like to make this soup in late summer when all vegetables are fresh except peas. I also like ground turkey because it has little fat. My family looks forward to this summer delight.

— *Ethel Stoner, John R. Stoner Vegetables*

# Ham Vegetable Chowder

*Makes 10 – 12 servings*

2 cups ham, cubed
2 medium onions, chopped
5 cups potatoes, cubed
1½ cups water
1 quart milk

2 Tbsp. butter
2 Tbsp. flour
¼ tsp. baking soda
6-oz. can tomato paste
1 cup corn

1. Combine ham, onion, potatoes and water. Cook until soft, then add milk.
2. In a large separate pan melt butter and flour, baking soda and tomato paste. Heat, stirring until smooth.
3. Add ham mixture and corn and bring to a boil. Serve.

— *Linda Kauffman, Sallie Y. Lapp*

◆

# Veal Shin Soup

2 – 3 lb. veal shin
¼ cup carrots, diced
¼ cup potatoes, diced
¼ cup celery, diced
2 Tbsp. parsley

2 Tbsp. flour
2 Tbsp. butter
¼ tsp. cloves
½ tsp. allspice
1 hard-boiled egg, diced

1. Cook veal and remove from bone. Cook carrots, potatoes, celery and parsley in veal broth until vegetables are soft.
2. Brown flour in butter and add to soup. Add cloves, allspice and diced hard-boiled egg.

*—Roberta B. Peters, Pennsylvania Dutch Gifts*

# Homemade Chicken Corn Soup

*Makes 12 – 16 servings*

4 – 5 lb. roaster chicken
6 cups chicken broth
6 cups water
1 can yellow corn (substitute 3 ears fresh)
1 can white corn (substitute 3 ears fresh)
4 hard-boiled eggs, diced
1 Tbsp. dried parsley or 3 sprigs fresh
6 ozs. medium noodles
salt and pepper to taste
saffron (a pinch plus)
1 cup boiling water

1. Cook chicken in about 8 cups water. When chicken is cooked, remove from broth and cool. Remove fat from chicken broth. Chop chicken.
2. Place chopped chicken, 6 cups broth and 6 cups water in a 6-quart kettle.
3. Pour boiling water over saffron. Set aside. Hot water will draw out golden yellow coloring and flavoring.
3. Add drained corn, eggs and parsley to chicken. Crumble noodles into kettle and salt and pepper to taste. Add saffron water. Stir and simmer until hot.

Great way to use up leftover chicken. It is so good! In fact, the soup improves as it ages, so don't eat it all at the first sitting.

*—Brad Loercher, Parsley Porch*

# Creamy Crab Meat Soup

*Makes 4 – 6 servings*

| | |
|---|---|
| 1 lb. claw crab meat | 1 Tbsp. flour |
| 2 hard-boiled eggs | 1 quart rich milk |
| rind of 1 lemon, grated | ½ cup cream |
| 1 Tbsp. butter, melted | ½ cup sherry |

1. Pick over crab meat and remove any shell. Place in a deep mixing bowl.
2. Chop eggs finely and add to crab. Blend well and add lemon rind, butter and flour.
3. Blend well and add milk. Pour mixture into top of double boiler. Place over boiling water. Heat thoroughly. Remove from heat.
4. Add cream. Heat and season with sherry.
5. Serve in hot bowls.
> — *Charles Fox and Larry McElhenny, New Holland Sea Food*

# Fish Chowder

*Makes 6 – 8 servings*

| | |
|---|---|
| 1 lb. haddock fillet | 1 bay leaf, crumbled |
| 2 cups water | 2 cups milk |
| 2 – 3 large potatoes, diced | 1 Tbsp. butter |
| 1 oz. bacon | 1 tsp. salt |
| 1 onion, sliced | few grains pepper |
| ½ cup celery, diced | |

1. Simmer haddock in water for 15 minutes. Drain, reserving broth.
2. Cook potatoes in broth until almost soft.
3. Sauté bacon until crisp. Remove from pan. In bacon drippings sauté celery and onion until golden brown.
4. Crumble fish. Add fish, onion, celery and bay leaf to potatoes and broth.
5. Add milk and butter and simmer 5 minutes. Salt and pepper to taste.
6. Pour into serving dish and top with crumbled bacon.
> — *Helen E. Bitner, Bitners*

# Corn Chowder

*Makes 6 servings*

4 Tbsp. onion, chopped
3 Tbsp. butter
4 cups milk
2 cups potatoes, boiled

2 cups stewed corn
1½ tsp. salt
⅛ tsp. pepper
few grains cayenne pepper

1. Sauté onion in butter until a delicate brown. Add milk, potatoes, corn, salt, pepper and cayenne pepper. Bring soup to a boil and simmer for about 5 minutes.
2. Serve a cracker in each portion of soup.
— *Nancy Geib, Nancy's Goodies*

# Cheese and Corn Chowder

*Makes 6 servings*

2 cups potatoes, diced
1 cup carrots, sliced
1 cup celery, chopped
½ cup water
1 tsp. salt

¼ tsp. pepper
2 cups creamed corn
1½ cups milk
⅔ cup cheese, grated

1. Put potatoes, carrots and celery into water. Add salt and pepper and simmer for 10 minutes covered.
2. Add creamed corn and simmer 5 more minutes.
3. Add milk and cheese. Stir over heat until cheese melts and chowder is heated through. Do not bring to a boil. Serve.
— *Miriam M. Hess, Frank Weaver Greenhouses*

# Creamy Cheese Soup

*Makes 4 – 6 servings*

2 cups water
1 cup carrots, shredded
1 medium onion, chopped
½ cup celery, chopped
1 tsp. salt
2 dashes Tabasco® sauce

8-oz. pkg. cream cheese, cut up
2 cups milk
2 Tbsp. butter or margarine, softened
2 Tbsp. flour
parsley

1. In 3-quart saucepan combine water, carrots, onion, celery, salt and Tabasco® sauce. Bring to a boil, reduce heat and cook covered 15 minutes or until vegetables are tender.

2. Stir in cream cheese until melted. Add milk. Blend butter and flour together and add to saucepan. Cook and stir until mixture thickens and bubbles.
3. Garnish each serving with snipped parsley.

*—Ethel Stoner, John R. Stoner Vegetables*

# Minestrone

*Makes 6 – 8 servings*

| | |
|---|---|
| 1 cup celery, chopped | 2 6-oz. cans tomato paste |
| 1 cup onion, chopped | 1 cup cabbage, chopped |
| 1 clove garlic, minced | 10-oz. pkg. peas and carrots |
| ¼ cup oil | 1 quart beef broth |
| 2½ tsp. salt | 2 cups kidney beans |
| ½ tsp. pepper | 1 cup macaroni, uncooked |
| 2 quarts water | |

1. Cook celery, onion and garlic in oil. Add all other ingredients except kidney beans and macaroni and simmer 1 hour.
2. Add kidney beans and macaroni and simmer another 15 minutes.

Different. Tasty and nutritious vegetable soup!

*—Thelma Thomas, Willow Valley Farms*

# Cream of Vegetable Soup

*Makes 6 – 8 servings*

| | |
|---|---|
| 1 cup potatoes, diced | 4 Tbsp. butter |
| 1 cup carrots, diced | 2 Tbsp. flour |
| ¾ cup celery, diced | 3 cups milk |
| 3 cups hot water | 2 tsp. salt |

1. Cook vegetables in water until soft.
2. Melt butter in saucepan and add flour and blend well. Add milk and cook until thickened, stirring constantly.
3. Add vegetables with their liquid to the white sauce. Add salt and heat until mixture is hot. Serve hot.

*—Joyce Deiter, Eisenberger's Baked Goods*

**Variation:**
1. Add ½ cup chopped onions to the vegetables and cook until soft.
2. Add a sprinkling of your favorite herbs, plus paprika and parsley before the final heating of the soup.

◆

# Cheesy Broccoli Bisque

*Makes 3 – 4 servings*

1 cup onion, chopped
1 cup mushrooms,
   sliced
3 Tbsp. margarine or
   butter
3 Tbsp. flour
1 – 2 tsp. garlic powder

3 cups chicken broth
1 cup broccoli flowerets
1 cup light cream or evaporated
   skim milk
1 cup Jarlsberg or Swiss cheese,
   shredded

1. In large saucepan sauté onion and mushroom in margarine until tender. Add flour and cook, stirring until bubbly. Add garlic powder.
2. Remove from heat and gradually add chicken broth. Return to heat. Cook, stirring until thickened and smooth.
3. Add broccoli, reduce heat and simmer 20 minutes or until vegetables are tender.
4. Blend in cream and cheese. Simmer until heated thoroughly and cheese is melted.

*—Ethel Stoner, John R. Stoner Vegetables*

# Cream of Broccoli Soup

*Makes 4 servings*

¼ cup onion, finely chopped
¼ cup celery, finely chopped
¼ cup margarine or butter
3 Tbsp. flour
¼ tsp. salt

dash pepper
1½ cups chicken broth
1½ cups milk
2 cups broccoli, cooked and
   drained
2 tsp. lemon juice
¼ tsp. garlic powder

1. In medium saucepan sauté onion and celery in margarine until tender. Stir in flour, salt and pepper. Cook 1 minute, stirring constantly until smooth and bubbly.
2. Gradually stir in chicken broth and milk. Cook until slightly thickened, stirring constantly. Do not boil.
3. Add chopped broccoli, lemon juice and garlic powder. Heat gently, stirring frequently.

*—Barbara Finefrock, Willow Valley Farms*

# Cream of Asparagus Soup

*Makes 4 – 6 servings*

1 bunch asparagus
3 Tbsp. butter
1 small onion, diced
3 cups chicken stock
1 small potato, diced

8-oz. pkg. cream cheese
1 tsp. salt
1 tsp. pepper
1 Tbsp. chives
½ cup Parmesan cheese

1. Cut asparagus into 1-inch pieces. Reserve several spears for garnish.
2. Melt butter and sauté onion until tender. Add chicken stock and cook asparagus and potatoes until potatoes are fork tender.
3. Purée broth and vegetables with cream cheese in blender or food processor.
4. Return mixture to cooking pot and season. Add Parmesan cheese.
5. Serve hot and garnish with asparagus spears.

— *Pam Griffe, The Goodie Shoppe*

# Arugula Soup

*Makes 4 – 6 servings*

2 cups arugula leaves
1 lb. potatoes
1 lb. leeks
2 quarts water plus 2 tsp. bouillon

1 tsp. salt
⅛ tsp. pepper
½ tsp. garlic powder
½ cup heavy cream (optional)

1. Wash and dry arugula and set aside. Peel potatoes and dice. Wash leeks and slice white portion.
2. Combine leeks and potatoes with water and bouillon. Simmer 25 minutes until tender. Add arugula and cook 10 minutes.
3. Put into blender or food processor and purée. Add seasonings. Add cream, if desired. Serve immediately.

Although arugula is used mostly as a salad green, it can also be cooked in a variety of ways as in this soup recipe.

— *Ethel Stoner, John R. Stoner Vegetables*

**Variation:**
Use 2 quarts chicken broth instead of water and bouillon.

# Potato Soup

*Makes 6 servings*

6 slices bacon
¼ cup onion, chopped
2 medium potatoes
1 cup water

¾ tsp. salt
2 cans cream of chicken soup
2½ cups milk
2 Tbsp. parsley flakes

1. Snip bacon into small pieces. In large saucepan cook until crisp. Set bacon aside. Reserve 3 Tbsp. bacon drippings. Add onions and cook slightly.
2. Dice potatoes. Add water, potatoes and salt to cooked onions and cook until tender, about 10 minutes.
3. Mash potatoes slightly, if desired. Blend undiluted soup and milk into potatoes and heat mixture. Do not bring to a boil. Add bacon and parsley flakes and serve.

Easy to make and has a great flavor!
— *Mary Lou Graby, Spring Glen Farm Kitchens, Inc.*

**Variation:**
For the calorie-conscious, use bacon bits instead of bacon and skim milk instead of whole milk.

# Potato Leek Soup

*Makes 4 – 6 servings*

3 medium leeks
4 medium potatoes, cubed
4 carrots, grated
2 cups chicken stock

⅛ tsp. pepper
2 cups skim milk
parsley to garnish

1. Cut roots off leeks and discard their tough outer leaves. Cut each leek in half lengthwise. Rinse thoroughly with cold running water.
2. Cut white part of leeks and enough of green tops into ¼-inch slices to make 2 cups.
3. Put leeks, potatoes and carrots into 3-quart saucepan with enough water to cover and cook over high heat until tender.
4. Add chicken stock. When heated thoroughly, add milk and pepper. Heat to serve. Garnish with parsley before serving.
— *Ethel Stoner, John R. Stoner Vegetables*

# Sauerkraut Soup

*Makes 4 servings*

1 pkg. dried onion soup mix
16-oz. can stewed tomatoes
½ lb. sauerkraut
salt and pepper to taste
1 loaf French or German bread

1. Prepare dried onion soup as directed on the box. Add the stewed tomatoes. Add sauerkraut and season to taste. Heat until piping hot.
2. Serve with crusty French or German bread.

I created this recipe after tasting at similar soup at a German inn in north-central Pennsylvania on a cold snowy night.
— *Barbara J. Weaver, D. M. Weaver and Sons, Inc.*

# Pumpkin Cream Soup

*Makes 6 servings*

1½ tsp. onion, chopped
3 Tbsp. butter
2½ Tbsp. flour
2¼ cups pumpkin purée
4½ cups chicken broth
1½ tsp. salt
¾ tsp. ginger
¼ tsp. nutmeg
white pepper to taste
3 egg yolks, slightly beaten
1½ cups evaporated milk
  (substitute skim milk)
¼ cup parsley

1. Sauté onion in butter until tender. Stir in flour and cook over low heat. Remove from heat.
2. Add pumpkin purée, broth, salt, ginger, nutmeg and pepper. Return to heat and stir with whisk until sauce is thick and smooth.
3. Combine egg yolks with milk and add to mixture. Bring to boiling point, stirring constantly. Do not allow to boil.
4. Correct seasoning and add chopped parsley.
— *Ethel Stoner, John R. Stoner Vegetables*

# SALADS AND RELISHES

# Hot Chicken Salad

*Makes 12 servings*

3 lbs. chicken
1 cup rice
1 cup celery, diced
¾ cup mayonnaise
½ cup blanched chopped
   onions
1 can cream of chicken soup
3 hard-boiled eggs, chopped
2-oz. jar pimentos
2 Tbsp. green peppers,
   chopped

1 Tbsp. onion, chopped
1 Tbsp. lemon juice
¼ tsp. salt
1 small can sliced water
   chestnuts
½ – 1 cup buttered bread
   crumbs

1. Cook chicken, cool and cut off bones. Chop into small pieces.
2. Cook rice according to directions.
3. Mix all ingredients except bread crumbs and spoon into a greased casserole. Top with bread crumbs.
4. Bake at 350° for 45 minutes.

My daughter-in-law, who is a wonderful cook, made this for our first meal together.

— *Viv Hunt, Viv's Varieties*

# Red Beet Eggs

*Makes 1 dozen eggs*

12 eggs
½ cup brown sugar
½ cup granulated sugar
½ tsp. salt

¼ cup water
¾ cup vinegar
1 quart canned red beets
   and juice

1. Cover eggs with lukewarm water in a saucepan. Heat until water comes to a full boil. Remove from heat and let stand in water for 20 minutes. Run cold water over eggs to cool them quickly. Peel eggs.
2. Mix brown sugar, granulated sugar, salt, water and vinegar and heat until sugar is dissolved, stirring occasionally. Add red beets and juice to this mixture and pour over the peeled eggs.
3. Refrigerate at least 12 hours.
4. Serve eggs sliced in half.

— *Joyce Deiter, Eisenberger's Baked Goods*

◆

# Stuffed Eggs

*Makes 12 halves*

6 eggs, hard boiled
2 Tbsp. mayonnaise
1 tsp. vinegar
¼ tsp. salt

dash of pepper
¼ tsp. paprika
½ tsp. mustard

1. Cut eggs in half and remove yolks. Set aside white parts of eggs.
2. Mash yolks and blend with all remaining ingredients. Use this mixture to fill the whites of the eggs. Serve.

— *Helen Thomas, Helen Thomas Produce*

# Blue Cheese Potato Salad

*Makes 6 – 8 servings*

2 lbs. new red potatoes, chopped into quarters
2 celery ribs, chopped
3 scallions, chopped
½ cup sour cream
½ cup mayonnaise
¼ cup Stilton (or your favorite blue cheese), crumbled
¼ cup fresh parsley, chopped
salt and pepper to taste

1. Put potatoes into boiling water. Cook for 15 minutes. Drain well. Salt potatoes while hot.
2. Combine all ingredients and serve.

Note: A good quality blue cheese is essential.

— *Kathleen Pianka, Marion Cheese*

# Seven Layer Salad

*Makes 8 – 10 servings*

1 large head lettuce
1 cup celery, chopped
¼ cup onion, chopped
½ lb. bacon, cooked and
   crumbled

1 small box frozen peas
6 hard-boiled eggs, sliced
1 cup light mayonnaise
8 ozs. cheese, shredded

1. Layer lettuce, celery, onion, bacon, peas and eggs in a glass bowl. Spread mayonnaise over salad. Sprinkle cheese on top.
2. Cover and refrigerate overnight.

— *Marilyn Denlinger, Irwin S. Widders Produce*

# Irish Tomato Salad

*Makes 4 – 8 servings*

| | |
|---|---|
| 1 small cucumber, chopped | ½ cup vegetable oil |
| 1 small green pepper, chopped | ¼ cup lemon juice |
| | 1 tsp. salt (optional) |
| 6 scallions and tops | 4 large tomatoes, thinly sliced |
| 6 Tbsp. fresh parsley | |
| ½ cup fresh mint | red leaf lettuce |

1. Mix together cucumber, green pepper, scallions, parsley and mint in blender for several seconds.
2. Add vegetable oil, beginning with a few tablespoons and using up to ½ cup, as preferred.
3. Add lemon juice and salt. Blend for several seconds. Pour mixture over tomato slices and let stand for 1 – 2 hours.
4. Arrange over red leaf lettuce and serve.

Beautiful, bright salad with a delicious taste! Goes especially well with pork, lamb or veal.

— *Grace Kauffman, Funk Brothers, Inc.*

# Sunshine Salad

*Makes 8 – 10 servings*

| Salad Ingredients: | Dressing Ingredients: |
|---|---|
| 1 bunch romaine lettuce | 1 cup cider vinegar |
| 2 bunches red leaf lettuce | 1 cup vegetable oil |
| ½ red onion | ½ cup honey |
| 2 avocados | 2 tsp. poppy seeds |
| 16 – 20 cherry tomatoes | salt and pepper to taste |

1. Wash lettuce and shake off excess water. Tear into bite-size pieces and place in a plastic bag with paper towel. Refrigerate overnight to crisp.
2. Put lettuce into a large bowl. Slice onion into thin pieces and add to salad. Peel and slice avocados and add to salad.
3. Add cherry tomatoes.
4. To prepare dressing mix all ingredients in a small bowl or jar and stir until well blended.
5. Pour dressing over salad and toss well. Season with salt and pepper.

Good anytime of year!

— *Doris Shenk, Donegal Gardens*

**Variation:**
Substitute mandarin oranges for cherry tomatoes.

◆

# Fresh Broccoli Salad

*Makes 8 servings*

**Salad Ingredients:**
3 strips bacon
1 large head broccoli
1 Tbsp. onion, minced
1 medium carrot, peeled
   and grated
¾ cup raisins
½ cup cashews (optional)

**Dressing Ingredients:**
1 cup mayonnaise
½ cup ganulated sugar or
   honey
2 Tbsp. vinegar

1. Mix all dressing ingredients and set aside for 1 hour.
2. Fry bacon strips, then crumble and set aside.
3. Prepare vegetables, cutting broccoli into bite-size pieces.
4. Toss bacon, vegetables, raisins and cashews together. Pour dressing over salad and serve immediately.

I like when my family eats foods with bulk and fiber. This is one way to get these foods into their diet, and they like it.

— *Ruth Thomas, Helen Thomas Produce*

# Cauliflower Salad

*Makes 6 – 8 servings*

**Salad Ingredients:**
1 head cauliflower
½ lb. bacon
1 small onion, diced
8 ozs. cheese, grated
green lettuce or spinach

**Dressing Ingredients:**
1 cup salad dressing
½ cup sugar
2 Tbsp. vinegar

1. Clean cauliflower and cut into small flowerets. Fry bacon until it is crisp and crumble it. Mix cauliflower, bacon, onion and cheese together.
2. Blend all dressing ingredients, then pour over salad and toss lightly. Refrigerate several hours or overnight.
3. Serve on green lettuce or a spinach leaf.

Healthy, refreshing salad for anytime of year!

— *Edith R. Weaver, Frank Weaver Greenhouses*

# Pepper Cabbage

*Makes 10 – 12 servings*

**Salad Ingredients:**
8 cups cabbage, shredded
1 large red or green pepper,
    diced
1 cup celery, diced
1 carrot, shredded
¼ onion, shredded
salt to taste

**Dressing Ingredients:**
2 cups sugar
1 cup vinegar
½ cup water
1 tsp. celery seed
1 tsp. mustard seed

1. In a large bowl mix cabbage, pepper, celery, carrot and onion. Sprinkle with salt and toss.
2. Mix all dressing ingredients and bring to a boil. Boil for 1 minute. Cool until lukewarm. Pour dressing over salad and mix thoroughly.
3. This will keep well for a long time in a refrigerator.

*—Anna F. Kreider, Viv's Varieties*

# Tangy Cabbage Salad

*Makes 14 – 16 servings*

4 cups cabbage, chopped
1 cup pineapple chunks, drained
2 apples, peeled and chopped
½ cup walnuts, chopped
⅔ cup miniature marshmallows
⅔ cup mayonnaise
½ cup sugar
2 Tbsp. pineapple juice

1. Combine cabbage, pineapple chunks, apples, walnuts and marshmallows in a bowl.
2. Combine mayonnaise, sugar and pineapple juice. Mix well. Pour over other ingredients slowly. Mix well and chill.

Different. You don't realize you are eating cabbage.

*—Grace E. Baker, S. Clyde Weaver, Inc.*

# Green Bean Salad

*Makes 6 – 8 servings*

**Salad Ingredients:**
3 cups green beans, cooked
4 hard-boiled eggs
1 medium onion
1 large dill pickle

**Dressing Ingredients:**
2 Tbsp. vinegar
1 tsp. salt
⅔ cup mayonnaise

1. Chop green beans, eggs, onion and dill pickle and combine.
2. Mix together vinegar, salt and mayonnaise and pour over bean mixture. Stir gently.
3. Chill and serve.

— *Ruth Harnish, Spring Glen Farm Kitchens, Inc.*

# Black Bean Salad with Roasted Red Peppers

*Makes 4 – 6 servings*

2 can black beans, drained
1 red pepper, seeded and cut into slices
3 – 4 scallions, sliced
2 – 3 plum tomatoes, diced
6 Tbsp. olive oil
3 Tbsp. lemon juice
5 Tbsp. fresh cilantro, chopped
1 tsp. coarse black pepper
salt to taste
3 – 4 red peppers

1. Combine all ingredients except red peppers and toss in a glass bowl.
2. To prepare peppers hold 3 – 4 red peppers with tongs over a gas flame until skin is chafed. Place in paper bag and let steam. Peel, de-seed and slice into quarters. Sprinkle peppers with lemon juice and freshly ground pepper.
3. Garnish bean salad with pepper wedges and serve.

Beautiful, easy and nutritious!

— *Regine Ibold, The Spice Stand*

◆

# Carrot Salad

*Makes 3 – 4 servings*

| | |
|---|---|
| 6 – 8 carrot stalks | ½ cup vinegar |
| 1 green pepper | ½ cup oil |
| 1 medium onion | ¾ cup sugar |
| 1 can tomato soup | |

1. Slice carrots and cook in water until soft.
2. Dice pepper and onion and mix with soup, vinegar, oil and sugar.
3. Drain water off carrots and add to mixture. Refrigerate overnight and serve.

— *Roberta B. Peters, Pennsylvania Dutch Gifts*

# Gourmet Tossed Salad

*Makes 6 – 8 servings*

| *Salad Ingredients:* | *Dressing Ingredients:* |
|---|---|
| radicchio leaves | 2 – 3 tsp. shallots or scallions |
| arugula | ½ tsp. dry mustard |
| red leaf lettuce | ¼ tsp. salt |
| watercress | ⅛ tsp. freshly ground pepper |
| romaine lettuce | 1 Tbsp. wine vinegar |
| | 1 Tbsp. lemon juice |
| | ½ cup good quality olive oil |
| | 1 tsp. fresh parsley or dill |

1. Arrange on individual plates or in a salad bowl the following greens which have been washed and drained: radicchio leaves, arugula, red leaf lettuce, watercress and romaine lettuce.
2. Prepare a basic vinaigrette by combining all dressing ingredients. Shake together in a jar (or whisk) and pour over greens. Serve.

One of many unique things about Central Market is the availability of home-grown arugula and radicchio. My husband, John Stoner, started growing these greens within the last two years. Our customers especially enjoy arugula. Regine Ibold gave me this recipe and she should have the credit for it.

— *Ethel Stoner, John R. Stoner Vegetables*

◆

# Spinach Salad

*Makes 6 servings*

**Salad Ingredients:**
½ peck fresh spinach
¼ cup bacon bits
1 hard-boiled egg, chopped

**Dressing Ingredients:**
½ cup sugar
1 cup vegetable oil
⅓ cup ketchup
½ cup vinegar
1 medium onion, minced
2 Tbsp. Worcestershire® sauce

1. Combine all dressing ingredients and chill.
2. Tear spinach into small pieces and cover with dressing. Top with bacon bits and chopped egg.

*— Ruth Gerlach, Irwin S. Widders Produce*

# Spinach Salad With Hot Bacon Dressing

*Makes 6 servings*

**Dressing Ingredients:**
1 cup sugar
1 tsp. salt
1 tsp. cornstarch or flour
1 tsp. mustard
2 eggs, beaten
½ cup milk
½ cup vinegar
½ lb. bacon
1 tsp. bacon drippings

**Salad Ingredients:**
1 lb. spinach (washed and cut)
½ lb. mushrooms, sliced
8 hard-boiled eggs, sliced

1. Mix sugar, salt, cornstarch or flour and mustard in a blender. Add beaten eggs and mix again. Add milk and vinegar. Pour mixture into a saucepan and cook until thickened.
2. Fry bacon and add crumbled pieces to dressing. To enhance taste add bacon drippings.
3. Wash spinach in hot water to remove all sand. Garnish spinach with mushrooms and sliced eggs. Serve with hot dressing.

*— Marilyn Widders Denlinger, Irwin S. Widders Produce*

# ◆ Hot Wilted Greens

*Makes 4 servings*

**Fresh greens: dandelion, spinach, endive or lettuce (use one
    or more)**
**4 slices lean bacon**
**½ cup Maurer's Mustard Sauce***
**1 hard-boiled egg**

1. Clean greens, drain and tear into pieces.
2. Cut bacon into 1-inch pieces and fry to a crisp. Drain off all but
2 Tbsp. bacon drippings. Add mustard sauce to bacon and reserved drippings and heat through.
3. Add greens to hot mustard sauce and stir thoroughly until wilted.
4. Serve hot on dinner plate or salad dish. Garnish with hard-boiled
eggs.

I recently confirmed this old family recipe with my 92-year-old
mother.

*— Richard H. Maurer, Maurer's Sauce Spot*

* Maurer's Mustard Sauce is made by Kitchen Kettle Foods,
Inc. expressly for Maurer's Sauce Spot.

# Greens-Mustard Sauce Salad

*Makes 4 servings*

**Fresh greens (spinach, endive or lettuce)**
**2 tomatoes**
**2 hard-boiled eggs**
**8 large mushrooms**
**1 medium onion**
**2 slices bacon**
**¼ cup Maurer's Mustard Sauce***

1. Cut each tomato into 4 wedges. Slice eggs and mushrooms.
Chop onion. Mix together.
2. Fry bacon, drain off fat and slice into small pieces.
3. Add bacon and mustard sauce to salad and mix well. Serve on a
bed of greens.

*— Richard H. Maurer, Maurer's Sauce Spot*

* Maurer's Mustard Sauce is made by Kitchen Kettle Foods,
Inc. expressly for Maurer's Sauce Spot.

# Dandelion Greens With Hot Bacon Dressing

*Makes 6 – 8 servings*

| | |
|---|---|
| 5 strips lean bacon | ⅔ cup water |
| 3 Tbsp. flour | ⅓ cup vinegar |
| ½ cup brown sugar | 4 – 6 quarts dandelion greens |

1. Fry bacon and remove from pan. In this saucepan brown flour. Add brown sugar, water and vinegar. Heat until mixture thickens, stirring constantly.
2. Remove from heat and add crumbled bacon to mixture.
3. Fill a 6-quart kettle with cleaned dandelion greens and steam until tender. Drain.
4. Toss dressing and dandelion greens together and serve.

*— Sam Neff, S. Clyde Weaver, Inc.*

**Variation:**
Garnish with hard-boiled eggs.

## Gathering Dandelion Greens

Dandelion is one of those special vegetables that brings back many memories of growing up in Lancaster County. Hot Bacon Dressing is a traditional sweet and sour. The proportions of sugar and vinegar may be adjusted to the individual's preference. Generally, we in Lancaster enjoy more sour. The above recipe is medium.

Dandelion greens are a scavenger's delight (or you can buy them at Central Market). They must be gathered before flowering or the end result is too bitter and tough. Look along fence rows or at the edges of wooded areas. The large single clumps are easiest to clean. Cut the dandelion out of the ground with a knife. Cut at the root which is below the heart. This will keep the plant together when you wash the greens.

After gathering a nice shopping bag full, clean each plant under running water and remove dead leaves around exterior. Rinse thoroughly. Before putting the greens into a kettle for steaming, cut off the root and a bit of the heart so the leaves separate. The heart buds are also edible if not too large.

The season for dandelion greens is short, but I look forward to it every year. I make mental notes of where I see the flowers blooming in the spring and return to those spots the following March. I now live in the city of Lancaster and find that the cemeteries are great dandelion beds. This is especially true if they are fenced and have little pet traffic!

*— Sam Neff, S. Clyde Weaver, Inc.*

# Hommus Salad or Chick Pea Salad

*Makes 4 – 6 servings*

10-oz. can chick peas
¼ cup flat-leaf parsley,
  chopped
1 medium tomato, diced
1 clove garlic, chopped or
  pressed

pinch of salt and pepper
3 Tbsp. fresh lemon juice
4 Tbsp. olive oil

1. Boil chick peas until tender (about 3 – 5 minutes). Drain and combine with parsley, tomato, garlic, salt and pepper. Add lemon juice and olive oil.
2. Serve hot or cold.

Very filling, especially on cold days. Nutritious and economical.
— *Gary Alhusseini, Habibi's*

**Variation:**
For another dish called *foul m'dammas,* substitute broad beans for chick peas.

# Sour Cream Pineapple Salad

*Makes 4 – 6 servings*

6-oz. pkg. orange-flavored gelatin
3 cups boiling water
2 cups sour cream
1 cup nuts, chopped
2 cups crushed pineapple, drained

1. Dissolve gelatin in boiling water. Gradually add sour cream with a whisk.
2. Add nuts and pineapples and pour into a dish. Let stand until firm before serving.

— *Willow Valley Farms*

**Variation:**
Serve on lettuce leaves and garnish with mandarin oranges and whipped cream.

# Strawberry Pretzel Salad

*Makes 12 – 16 servings*

*Crush Ingredients:*
**2 cups pretzels, crushed**
**3 Tbsp. sugar**
**¾ cup butter or margarine, melted**

*Filling Ingredients:*
**8-oz. pkg. cream cheese**
**1 cup sugar**
**1 large container whipped topping**

*Topping Ingredients:*
**6-oz. pkg. strawberry gelatin**
**2 cups hot water**
**10-oz. pkg. frozen strawberries**
**1 can crushed pineapple, drained**

1. Mix all crust ingredients and press into a 9″ × 13″ pan. Bake at 400° for 7 minutes. Let cool.
2. Blend all filling ingredients and spread over crust.
3. To prepare topping dissolve gelatin in boiling water. Add frozen strawberries and pineapple. Chill about 45 minutes until mixture has thickened but not set. Pour over cream cheese layer.
4. Chill until set and ready to serve.

*—Miriam M. Hess, Frank Weaver Greenhouses*

# Rhubarb Salad

*Makes 8 servings*

**3 cups rhubarb, finely cut**          **1 cup celery, finely chopped**
**⅔ cup sugar**                          **2½ cups water**
**¼ tsp. salt**                          **1 Tbsp. lemon juice**
**⅓ cup water**                          **½ cup nuts, chopped**
**6-oz. pkg. strawberry gelatin**

1. Cook together rhubarb, sugar, salt and ⅓ cup water.
2. Add gelatin, celery, 2½ cups water, lemon juice and nuts. Mix well.
3. Chill until firm.

*—Joyce Fair, Utz's Potato Chips*

♦

# Cranberry Salad

*Makes 16 servings*

**Salad Ingredients:**
1 lb. cranberries
2 cups water
1 cup sugar
6-oz. pkg. cherry gelatin
2 cups red grapes, halved
  and seeded
20-oz. can crushed pineapple, undrained
1 cup nuts, chopped (op-
  tional)

**Topping Ingredients:**
8-oz. pkg. cream cheese
¼ cup milk
1 tsp. vanilla
2 cups whipped
  topping

1. Combine cranberries, water and sugar. Cook until cranberries pop. Remove from heat and add gelatin.
2. Add all remaining salad ingredients. Pour into a large bowl and chill at least 4 hours. Do not use a mold.
3. To prepare topping beat cream cheese, milk and vanilla until smooth. Fold in whipped topping.
4. Serve salad covered with topping.

—*Joanne Mylin, Irwin S. Widders Produce*

**Variation:**

Instead of fresh cranberries use two 16-oz. cans whole berry cranberry sauce. Omit sugar and reduce water to one cup. Instead of Step One, pour 1 cup boiling water over gelatin, stirring until dissolved. Add cranberry sauce, one can at a time, and stir until well mixed. Continue with Step Two.

I have always loved going to market. My dad would call us as he left the house to load the market truck. We had an understanding with him that if the kitchen light was on when he drove back past the house, he would wait for us to come out and go with him. My mother says we were "grouchy all day" if we did not make it out of bed in time to turn on that light.

—*Sam Neff, S. Clyde Weaver, Inc.*

# Cranberry Orange Salad

*Makes 8 servings*

6-oz. pkg. strawberry gelatin
1½ cups boiling water
16-oz. can jellied cranberry sauce
1 Tbsp. orange rind, grated
2 oranges, finely diced
⅔ cup pecans, chopped

1. Dissolve gelatin in boiling water.
2. Stir cranberry sauce with fork or whisk until smooth. Add to gelatin. Also add orange rind, blending well.
3. Chill until slightly thickened. Add oranges and pecans. Mix well.
4. Pour into 5-cup mold. Chill until firm (about 4 hours or overnight). Unmold onto a bed of lettuce.

A family favorite over the holidays.

—*Joyce Deiter, Eisenberger's Baked Goods*

# Apple Salad

*Makes 4 – 5 servings*

4 – 5 apples
½ – ¾ cup raisins
½ cup nuts
½ cup celery, diced

¾ cup mayonnaise or salad
  dressing
¼ cup milk
¼ cup sugar
sweetened vinegar (optional)

1. Dice apples. Add raisins, nuts and celery and mix well.
2. Combine mayonnaise, milk and sugar and blend well. A little sweetened vinegar may be added. Pour this combination over apple mixture and mix well.
3. Serve with lettuce.

—*Mrs. Aaron King, Kauffman's Fruit Farm*

**Variations:**

1. Use a combination of Red and Golden Delicious apples to add color and flavor.
2. Use lemon juice instead of vinegar.

# Mint Julie Peach Salad

*Makes 12 servings*

*Salad Ingredients:*

6-oz. pkg. lemon gelatin
1½ cups hot water
½ cup frozen lemonade
   concentrate, thawed
7-oz. bottle 7-Up

few drops mint flavoring
1 cup cantaloupe balls
1 cup seedless grapes, halved
2 cups fresh peaches, diced

*Topping Ingredients:*
½ pint heavy cream, whipped
4 ozs. cream cheese, softened
⅓ cup confectioner's sugar
1 tsp. vanilla
pecans, chopped

1. Dissolve gelatin in hot water. Add lemonade concentrate, 7-Up and mint flavoring. Chill until partially set.
2. Add all remaining salad ingredients. Chill in an oblong glass dish until firm.
3. To prepare topping beat all ingredients together until smooth.
4. When ready to serve, cut gelatin into squares and cover with topping. Sprinkle each piece with pecans.

*—Dorothy High, Robert S. Meck*

# Raspberry Jello Salad

*Makes 6 – 8 servings*

*Salad Ingredients:*
6 tart apples
6 heaping tsp. sugar
pinch of salt
1¼ cups water
¾ cup water
6-oz. pkg. raspberry gelatin

*Dressing Ingredients:*
½ cup mayonnaise
1 Tbsp. milk
2 – 3 tsp. sugar

1. Peel apples and dice them. Add sugar, salt and 1¼ cups water. Boil until apples are soft.
2. Add another ¾ cup water to mixture. Stir in gelatin while mixture is still hot. Chill until set.
3. Serve with dressing on the side.

*—Jane Brenneman, Brenneman Farm*

# The Curb Market

Early in the history of Lancaster, the space allotted for the town market became insufficient. In the 1820s, in order to relieve the situation, farmers were permitted to back their wagons up to the curbs along the streets and sell their wares directly from their vehicles or temporary stands. This assemblage of sellers became known as the curb market. In a sense, it was an outgrowth of the Central Market, but it developed as a distinct entity.

The curb market was not a random arrangement. City ordinances specified which areas of which streets could be used for marketing. The places were neither occupied by market wagons on a first-come first-served basis, nor were they free for the taking.

In 1818 the curb market occupied West King Street as far as Prince Street and the whole of Center Square. By 1845 it extended a block in each direction from the Center Square on King and Queen Streets. In 1898 the curb market changed its dimensions again. There were 57 spaces on East King Street, 35 on Duke Street and nine in Center Square. These spaces were auctioned off, the same as those in the market house.

During its final period the curb market extended from Center Square on East King Street to Duke, down Duke to Vine, and west on Vine to Prince where it reached almost to Orange Street. In the same areas, stores and businesses also rented space along the fronts of their buildings to the operators of smaller businesses and their "basket stands."

The rows of wagons with upturned shafts and the sumptuous displays of farm produce were somewhat of an early-day tourist attraction in Lancaster. The outdoor stands were favored by some marketers because of their cheaper rent, and many shoppers and sellers alike enjoyed the fresh air.

After the First World War, motor vehicles began replacing horse-drawn wagons at the curb market. Eventually it was the increased auto traffic in town that caused the curb market to be impractical and unsafe. On January 1, 1927, the city decreed that this colorful institution come to an end. The standholders were offered space in the Southern Market.

# Warm Raspberry Salad

*Makes 6 – 8 servings*

1 medium head romaine (substitute mix of salad greens)
1 small can water chestnuts, drained and sliced
½ tsp. cracked black pepper
3 Tbsp. walnut oil
½ cup slivered almonds
¾ lb. mushrooms, cleaned and sliced
¼ cup raspberry vinegar

1. Wash and tear salad greens. Combine with water chestnuts and season with pepper. Chill.
2. Heat walnut oil in large skillet. Add almonds and sauté over high heat for 1 – 2 minutes. Add sliced mushrooms and sauté another 2 minutes. Add raspberry vinegar and stir briefly.
3. Pour dressing over chilled greens and toss. Serve immediately.

This dish allows salad to be a more substantial part of a meal. It is tart and full of textures.

— *Cindy Cover, Marion Cheese*

# Grace's Chow Chow

*Makes 6 – 8 quarts*

1 quart cucumbers, diced
1 quart string beans, green
  or yellow
1 quart corn
1 quart celery
1 quart fresh lima beans
1 pint green peppers
1 pint red peppers
1 cup small onions (optional)

1 quart vinegar
3 cups sugar
1 cup water
½ tsp. turmeric
1 Tbsp. salt

1. Chop all vegetables to desired size. Cook each one separately until tender, but not soft. Drain vegetables and mix together.
2. Combine vinegar, sugar and water. Bring to a boil. Add turmeric and salt. Add all vegetables to hot liquid and bring to boiling point.
3. Pack into hot jars and seal.

Typically Pennsylvania Dutch! Looks like a quilt in a jar.

— *Grace Kauffman, Funk Brothers, Inc.*

**Variation:**
Use dried lima beans which have been soaked and cooked until they are just tender.

# Spiced Cantaloupe

*Makes 8 – 10 servings*

2 – 3 cups cantaloupe chunks
1 cup granulated sugar
½ cup water, or more
4 Tbsp. vinegar

½ tsp. salt
1 drop oil of cloves
1 drop oil of cinnamon

1. Prepare cantaloupe and cut into desired size. Be sure to select firm cantaloupe. Pack into quart jar.
2. Mix all other ingredients and bring to a boil. Pour hot syrup over cantaloupe in jar. Cold pack for 10 minutes in a canner.

I enjoyed spiced cantaloupe as a girl when my mother made them. Today I make them for my own family.

— *Arlene Leaman, S. Clyde Weaver, Inc.*

**Variatins:**

1. Multiply this recipe and do more than one jar at a time.
2. Eliminate oil of cloves and oil of cinnamon and have pickled cantaloupe instead of spiced cantaloupe.

# Ten-Day Pickles

*Makes 12 pints*

7 lbs. cucumbers (6 – 7"
   long, 1" thick)
½ cup salt
1 quart water
4 cups water
1 Tbsp. alum
1 cup vinegar

4 lbs. sugar
1 quart vinegar
3 cinnamon sticks (¼ oz.
   each)
2 Tbsp. celery seed
2 Tbsp. whole allspice

1. Slice cucumbers into ¾-inch pieces and place into large crock. Cover with a mixture of ½ cup salt and 1 quart water. Double liquid, if necessary.
2. Allow cucumbers to soak in this mixture for three days.
3. After third day drain and cover completely with cold water. Do this each day for days 4, 5 and 6.
4. On day 7 drain again and cook pickles in a solution of 4 cups water, alum and 1 cup vinegar. Bring to a boil and boil over low heat for 2 hours, covered.
5. After cooking drain and pour liquid away. Return pickles to crock.
6. Mix sugar, 1 quart vinegar, cinnamon sticks, celery seed and allspice and bring to a boil. Boil for 3 minutes. Pour hot liquid over pickles in crock.

7. On days 8 and 9 drain liquid and save it. Reheat liquid to boiling point and pour over pickles again.
8. On day 10 heat pickles and liquid to boiling. Place in jars and seal.
— *Ethel Stoner, John R. Stoner Vegetables*

# Zucchini Pepper Relish

*Makes 5 – 6 pints*

| | |
|---|---|
| **10 cups zucchini, chopped** | **3½ cups sugar** |
| **4 sweet peppers, chopped** | **2½ cups vinegar** |
| **4 cups onions, chopped** | **1 tsp. turmeric** |
| **⅓ cup salt** | **½ tsp. celery seed** |
| | **½ tsp. black pepper** |

1. Put zucchini, peppers and onions into a bowl. Add salt and refrigerate overnight. Drain and rinse in cold water.
2. Add all other ingredients to mixture and bring to a boil. Boil for 30 minutes and put into jars to seal.
— *Rebecca King, John R. Stoner Vegetables*

# Zucchini Relish

*Makes 4 – 5 pints*

| | |
|---|---|
| **8 cups zucchini, diced** | **1 cup cider vinegar** |
| **2 cups onions, sliced** | **1¾ cups sugar** |
| **1 Tbsp. salt** | **½ tsp. celery seed** |
| **½ cup sweet red pepper, diced** | **½ tsp. mustard seed** |

1. Mix zucchini, onion and salt in a bowl and set aside for 1 hour.
2. Mix all remaining ingredients in a saucepan and bring to a boil. Drain zucchini mixture and add to boiling liquid. Bring mixture back to a boil. Remove from heat and chill.

Note: This recipe may be canned while still hot, or it will keep in a refrigerator for at least two weeks. Great on a burger!
— *Jackie Parker, The Goodie Shoppe*

# Cranberry Relish

*Makes 8 – 10 servings*

1 orange
6 – 8 red skin apples
1 lb. frozen cranberries
1 can crushed pineapple
1 cup sugar

1. Peel orange and core apples. Grind cranberries, orange and apples together.
2. Add pineapple and sugar. Mix well.
3. Keeps well or it may be frozen.

— *Anna Mary Neff, S. Clyde Weaver, Inc.*

# Barbecue Relish

| | |
|---|---|
| 10 cucumbers | 4 cups cider vinegar |
| 15 green tomatoes | 2 Tbsp. flour |
| ½ cup salt | 1 tsp. turmeric |
| 2 green sweet peppers | 1 Tbsp. celery seed |
| 4 red sweet peppers | 1 tsp. mustard seed |
| 8 large onions | 1 tsp. mustard powder |
| 1 bunch celery | 6 cups granulated sugar |

1. Take center seeds out of cucumbers. Grind cucumbers and tomatoes (not too fine). Add ½ cup salt and let stand covered for ½ day. Strain off juice.
2. Add sweet peppers, onions and celery and put through a grinder. Pour into kettle and cover with cider vinegar. Add flour, turmeric, celery seed, mustard seed, mustard powder and sugar.
3. Boil mixture for 1 hour or longer until it thickens.
4. Sterilize jars, tops and lids. Fill pint jars to within ½ inch of top. Seal.

— *Ruth Widders, Irwin S. Widders Produce*

During the 1930s and 1940s, Lancaster's high-society women dressed up to shop on market. I loved to watch them with their mink stoles, hats and gloves as they bought flowers and produce from my mother. They would place their purchases in special market baskets and stroll down the aisle to make their next purchase.

— *Viv Hunt, Viv's Varieties*

# VEGETABLES

◆

# Potato Filling

*Makes 10 – 12 servings*

| | |
|---|---|
| 6 cups boiled potatoes | 1 cup celery, chopped |
| 3 eggs | ½ cup parsley, chopped |
| 1½ cups milk | salt and pepper to taste |
| 2 – 3 cups dry bread crumbs or cubes | small amount crushed saffron (optional) |
| ½ cup butter | ¼ cup water (optional) |
| ½ cup onions, chopped | |

1. Mash potatoes and add eggs, milk and bread crumbs. Mix well.
2. Sauté onions and celery lightly in butter. Add to potato mixture. Also add parsley and salt and pepper to taste.
3. Soak saffron in water and add to potato mixture, if desired.
4. Mix well and pour into a greased casserole. Bake at 350° for 45 minutes to 1 hour until golden brown.

Saffron is a seasoning used in Lancaster County to flavor chicken and other recipes made with chicken. It is the stamen of the saffron crocus flower. The best comes from Spain. I always use only a small amount.

*—Anna Mary Neff, S. Clyde Weaver, Inc.*


# Gourmet Potatoes

*Makes 8 servings*

| | |
|---|---|
| 6 large potatoes | 1 cup sour cream |
| ¼ cup butter or margarine, melted | 1 tsp. salt |
| ⅓ cup onion, chopped | ¼ tsp. pepper |
| 1 – 2 cups cheddar cheese, shredded | paprika |

1. Cook potatoes in skins. Cool, peel and shred coarsely.
2. In a saucepan sauté onion in butter, Do not brown.
3. Fold potatoes, onion, cheese and sour cream together. Add salt and pepper. Sprinkle with paprika.
4. Place in a greased casserole dish and bake at 350° for 25 minutes.

May be made ahead of time and frozen.

*—Rose Meck, Robert S. Meck*
*—Mrs. Robert Funk, Funk Brothers, Inc.*

# Scalloped Potatoes

*Makes 8 servings*

8 medium potatoes  
1 medium onion, diced  
8 slices bacon, diced  
½ cup flour  

1 tsp. salt  
¼ tsp. pepper  
1 cup milk, or less  

1. Wash and peel potatoes. Cut into thin slices. In a greased casserole dish layer potatoes, onion, bacon, flour, salt and pepper. Repeat layers. Make sure there is a 2-inch space between top layer and top of casserole dish.
2. Pour enough milk over potatoes to almost cover potatoes.
3. Bake at 350° for 1 hour or until done. Stir once while baking.

Note: To prevent casserole from cooking over, always use raw bacon and an uncovered dish. Fat from the bacon keeps the milk from boiling over.

The Pennsylvania Dutch like their meat and potato meals. We grow potatoes so we often serve them.

— *Ruth Thomas, Helen Thomas Produce*

# Sweet Potato Croquettes

*Makes 40 large croquettes*

12 lbs. sweet potatoes  
¾ cup butter or margarine, melted  
3 tsp. salt  
½ cup brown sugar  
½ tsp. black pepper  
5 eggs, beaten  
2–3 cups bread crumbs  
1 cup vegetable oil  

1. Cook sweet potatoes until soft. Drain and peel them. Mash either by hand or with an electric mixer. Add margarine, salt, sugar and pepper. Mix well and refrigerate overnight.
2. Form mixture into croquettes in the shape of a small egg. Dip each croquette in beaten egg and then into the crumbs. Fry in the oil, turning until evenly browned. Do not let them get too dark.
3. Lay on cookie sheet lined with waxed paper and freeze. After croquettes are frozen, package and store in freezer.
4. To serve heat in 325° degree oven for 20 minutes.

Easy last minute meal when prepared ahead of time.

— *Ruth Widders, Irwin S. Widders Produce*

◆

# Baked Corn

*Makes 6 servings*

2 cups corn, cooked
1 cup milk
⅔ cup cracker or bread
   crumbs
3 Tbsp. butter, melted

½ tsp. salt
⅛ tsp. pepper
1 Tbsp. sugar
2 eggs
1 tsp. minced onion

1. Combine all ingredients in a blender and mix lightly.
2. Pour into a greased 1-quart casserole dish and bake at 350° for 40 minutes.

Grandma used to make this for us when we went there for dinner.
   *— Louella E. Groff, C. Z. Martin Sons*
   *— Rebecca King, John R. Stoner Vegetables*

**Variations:**
   1. Use 2½ cups cream-style corn plus 1 Tbsp. flour instead of whole-kernel corn. To bake, place casserole in a large pan with 1 inch of water.
   2. Use 2½ cups frozen corn. Thaw and add 2 Tbsp. flour to thicken corn.

This is a real comfort food. My two grown sons always want me to make corn pudding when they come home for a meal.
   *— Grace Kauffman, Funk Brothers, Inc.*

# Corn Fritters

*Makes 4 servings*

2 eggs
½ cup milk
1 pint corn, drained
½ cup flour, sifted
1 tsp. baking powder

1 tsp. salt
1 tsp. sugar
1 tsp. oil
½ cup cooking oil

1. Beat eggs and stir in milk.
2. Add corn and beat in flour, baking powder, salt, sugar and oil.
3. Heat cooking oil by tablespoonfuls as needed in a saucepan.
Drop corn mixture by tablespoonfuls into hot oil. Turn to brown.
Drain and serve hot.
   *— Ruth Widders, Irwin S. Widders Produce*

**Variation:**
   Serve with maple sugar or powdered sugar.

# Corn Pie

*Makes 1 9" pie*

| | |
|---|---|
| 2 cups fresh corn | 1 tsp. sugar |
| ½ cup milk | 1 Tbsp. parsley, chopped |
| 1 Tbsp. butter | 2 hard-boiled eggs, diced |
| 1 tsp. salt | 1 9" double unbaked pie crust |

1. Line 9-inch pie pan with pie shell.
2. Heat corn with milk and butter. Remove from heat and carefully stir in remaining ingredients. Place corn mixture in pie pan.
3. Cover top with pastry. Prick top with fork.
4. Bake at 400° for 10 minutes. Reduce oven temperature to 325° and bake an additional 35 minutes. Serve hot.

— *Cynthia Strube, Marion Cheese*

# Indian Corn Custard

*Makes 4 – 6 servings*

| | |
|---|---|
| 1⅓ cups summer squash, cooked and well drained | 2 Tbsp. flour |
| ¼ cup sugar | 2 large eggs, separated |
| ½ tsp. vanilla extract | ¼ tsp. cream of tartar |
| ½ cup corn | pinch of salt |
| | ¼ cup sugar |

1. Mash the squash (or use blender) until smooth. Add ¼ cup sugar, vanilla, corn and flour and mix thoroughly.
2. Combine mixture with egg yolks until well blended.
3. Beat egg whites until stiff. Fold in cream of tartar, salt and ¼ cup sugar and beat until peaks form. Fold meringue into custard until well blended.
4. Lightly grease and flour the bottom of an 8" cake pan or a 1-quart casserole and pour custard into dish.
5. Bake at 350° for 30 – 40 minutes or until lightly browned.

Squash grows well in this part of the country, but I find few recipes that use squash. I developed this one by myself. First, I came up with a product somewhat the consistency of a soufflé. After several changes, it became a custard dish. Corn was added to give the recipe texture. I find this a very satisfying recipe, especially on a cold winter day.

— *Sonia A. Miller, Michael's Homestyle Breads*

# Green Beans Supreme

*Makes 4 – 6 servings*

**4 slices bacon**
**¼ cup onion, chopped**
**1 can cream of celery or mushroom soup**
**⅓ cup milk**
**1 lb. fresh green beans or two 9-oz. pkgs. frozen green beans**

1. Cook bacon until crisp in a saucepan. Remove bacon and crumble.
2. Sauté onion in 2 Tbsp. bacon drippings until tender. Blend in soup, milk and green beans. Heat, stirring occasionally.
3. Top with bacon and serve.

*—Deb Martin, Martin's Home-Baked Goods*

# Spicy Green Beans

*Makes 6 servings*

**3 cups tomatoes, chopped**
**2 Tbsp. onion, minced**
**2 Tbsp. celery, diced**
**1 Tbsp. sugar**
**½ tsp. oregano**
**1 bay leaf**
**½ tsp. chili powder**
**dash of red pepper**
**½ tsp. garlic salt**
**⅛ tsp. cloves**
**⅛ tsp. pepper**
**2 Tbsp. flour**
**½ cup water**
**1 quart canned green beans**
**½ cup buttered bread crumbs**
**¼ cup cheese, grated**

1. Mix tomatoes, onions, celery, sugar and all spices. Simmer 15 minutes.
2. Mix flour with water to form a liquid paste. Add to tomato mixture and cook until thickened.
3. Pour green beans into a casserole dish. Pour tomato mixture over beans. Top with bread crumbs and grated cheese.
4. Bake at 350° for 1 hour.

*—Sara Jane Wenger, Tom's Flower Garden*

> **In the days before refrigeration, meat did not stay fresh all day. I remember how the bacon used to feel at the end of a long hot day. It was very much like open-air markets you see today in some other countries.**
> *—Paul L. and Anna Mary Neff, S. Clyde Weaver, Inc.*

# Barbecued Lima Beans

*Makes 6 – 8 servings*

¾ cup onion, chopped
½ – 1 cup brown sugar
1 cup ketchup
⅔ cup dark corn syrup
1 large can dried white lima
   beans

1 tsp. salt
1 Tbsp. liquid smoke
9 drops Tabasco® sauce
½ lb. bacon slices, browned

1. Combine onion, sugar, ketchup and syrup. Drain lima beans and stir into mixture. Add seasonings.
2. Brown bacon and crumble it. Add bacon to bean mixture.
3. Pour into casserole and bake uncovered at 400° for 1 hour or until beans are bubbly hot.

—*Ethel Stoner, John R. Stoner Vegetables*

# Scalloped Carrots

*Makes 8 – 10 servings*

12 medium carrots
4 Tbsp. butter
4 Tbsp. flour
1½ cups milk
¼ cup onions, chopped

¼ Tbsp. celery salt
½ cup cheese, diced
1 tsp. mustard
⅛ tsp. pepper
½ cup crushed potato chips

1. Dice carrots and cook until tender, but not too soft.
2. Make a white sauce by melting butter over medium heat. Add flour and stir until well mixed. Slowly add milk, stirring constantly.
3. Add onions, celery salt, cheese, mustard and pepper. Pour carrots and sauce into a baking dish. Top with crushed potato chips.
4. Bake at 350° for 45 minutes.

—*Mary Ellen Speicher, Sallie Y. Lapp*

# Baked Carrots

*Makes 8 – 10 servings*

10 – 12 carrots
1 can cream of celery soup
3 – 4 slices cheese
¼ lb. butter or margarine
1 cup dry bread crumbs

1. Prepare carrots by cleaning them and cutting them diagonally into ½-inch slices. Cook until just soft. Drain. Place in a 1-quart, greased casserole dish and add celery soup. Cover with cheese slices.
2. Melt butter and mix bread crumbs with melted butter. Put bread crumbs on top of cheese slices.
3. Bake at 325° approximately 20 – 25 minutes.

*—Dorothy High, Robert S. Meck*

# Ginger Lime Carrots

*Makes 8 – 10 servings*

3 lbs. carrots, peeled and
   sliced
3 cups water
1½ tsp. salt (optional)
2 Tbsp. butter
2 Tbsp. honey

2 Tbsp. fresh lime juice
1 Tbsp. peel of lime, grated
1 Tbsp. fresh ginger root,
   grated
lime slices

1. Cook carrots for 10 minutes in 3 cups salt water. Drain water from carrots.
2. Heat butter, honey, lime juice, lime peel and ginger in a sauce-pan for 5 minutes.
3. Pour glaze over carrots and stir until well glazed.
4. Put carrots in serving dish and garnish with lime slices.

*—Sam Neff, S. Clyde Weaver, Inc.*

# Cheese and Honey Glazed Carrots

*Makes 4 – 6 servings*

6 large carrots
salt to taste
¼ cup honey
1 cup cheese, shredded

1. Peel carrots and cut in half crosswise. Cook in a small amount of boiling salt water until carrots are tender (about 15 minutes). Do not overcook.

2. Drain and place carrots in a greased baking dish. Drizzle with honey. Sprinkle shredded cheese over carrots.
3. Bake at 400° for 10 minutes, or broil until cheese melts.
*—Deb Martin, Martin's Home-Baked Goods*

# Scalloped Asparagus

*Makes 8 servings*

1½ – 2 lbs. asparagus
6 Tbsp. butter
6 Tbsp. flour
1 tsp. salt
⅛ tsp. pepper

2 cups milk
¾ cup mild or sharp cheese, grated
2 Tbsp. onion, chopped
5 hard-boiled eggs, sliced
½ cup buttered bread crumbs

1. Steam asparagus until just tender. Drain and set aside.
2. Make a white sauce by melting butter. Stir in flour and add salt and pepper. Add milk, stirring constantly, and cook over low heat until smooth. Blend in ½ cup grated cheese, stirring until smooth.
3. Combine white sauce with asparagus, onion and eggs. Pour mixture into a 1½-quart greased casserole. Top with crumbs and remaining ¼ cup cheese.
4. Bake at 350° for 15 – 20 minutes or until casserole is bubbly and cheese melts.
*—Ruth Widders, Irwin S. Widders Produce*

# Creamed Asparagus

*Makes 4 – 6 servings*

2 lb. fresh asparagus
1 can asparagus soup
½ cup half and half
1 tsp. lemon juice

2 eggs, beaten
¼ cup blanched almonds
pasta shells or toast

1. Cut asparagus into ½-inch pieces. Cook in boiling water until crispy tender. Drain.
2. Combine soup, half and half, juice and eggs in a saucepan and heat thoroughly. Add asparagus and almonds to mixture.
3. Serve with pasta shells or toast.
*—Ethel Stoner, John R. Stoner Vegetables*

**Variation:**
Substitute evaporated skim milk for half and half.

# Pea Pot Pie

*Makes 8 – 10 servings*

4 cups flour
1 Tbsp. shortening, softened
3 eggs
1 tsp. salt

1 Tbsp. vinegar
½ cup water
1 quart peas, covered with water

1. Make a well in the flour. Put shortening, eggs, salt and vinegar into the well. Work into a stiff dough, adding water as needed to make dough good and stiff.
2. Roll dough out as thin as possible. Cut into 1-inch squares.
3. Cook peas, bringing to a boil. Drop pieces of pot pie into boiling water with peas. Cook about 4 to 5 minutes longer.

—*Mary E. Hess, Charles Hess*

# Roast Cabbage and Beef

*Makes 6 – 8 servings*

*Cabbage Ingredients:*
½ lb. beef cubes
1 small head cabbage
salt and pepper to taste
saffron (optional)
4 medium potatoes
4 medium apples
1 green pepper, chopped

*Bread Dressing Ingredients:*
6 – 8 slices bread, cubed
2 eggs, beaten
1 cup milk
1 tsp. parsley
1 tsp. onion
1 tsp. poultry seasoning

1. Partially cook beef cubes in water. Save broth.
2. Put ½ head cabbage, leaves separated, in bottom of roast pan. Add salt, pepper and saffron.
3. Layer beef cubes over cabbage.
4. Mix all ingredients for bread dressing, and layer over beef cubes in roast pan.
5. Repeat cabbage layer. Put apple slices around edge of pan and raw, cubed potatoes in center. Layer peppers over potatoes.
6. Pour broth from beef cubes over dish for moisture.
7. Bake covered at 300° for 2 hours.

I received this recipe from Mary Lauver after enjoying it at her house.

—*Helen Thomas, Helen Thomas Produce*

# Cabbage Bundles

*Makes 6 – 8 servings*

1 medium head cabbage
1½ lbs. hamburger
2 cups cooked rice

salt and pepper to taste
garlic salt
2 – 3 cups tomato juice or
    spaghetti sauce

1. Boil whole head of cabbage for 10 – 12 minutes. Separate leaves and set aside.
2. Brown hamburger. Blend rice and hamburger and season to taste.
3. Spoon about 2 Tbsp. mixture into each cabbage leaf. Roll leaves and hold with toothpicks. Place in greased baking dish and cover with tomato juice or spaghetti sauce. Bake at 350° for 1 hour, or steam in an electric frying pan for 1 hour.

*— Doris Shenk, Donegal Gardens*

# Brussels Sprouts Sauté

*Makes 4 servings*

3 Tbsp. butter
2 large carrots, sliced
2 cups Brussels sprouts,
    halved
1 medium leek, sliced
1 Tbsp. water

¼ tsp. caraway seeds
¼ tsp. salt
⅛ tsp. pepper
sour cream (optional)

1. Melt butter in a large skillet over medium heat. Sauté carrots for 3 minutes. Stir in Brussels sprouts and leeks and sauté 2 more minutes.
2. Add water. Cover and steam for 5 minutes or until Brussels sprouts are crisp and tender. Add additional water, if necessary.
3. Sprinkle with caraway seeds, salt and pepper. Serve with a dollop of sour cream, if you wish.

This vegetable combination has a wonderful flavor!

*— Funk Brothers, Inc.*

# Eggplant Creole

*Makes 4 – 6 servings*

1 medium eggplant
3 Tbsp. butter or margarine
3 Tbsp. flour
3 large tomatoes or 2 cups
   canned tomatoes
1 small green pepper,
   chopped
1 small onion, chopped

1 tsp. salt
1 Tbsp. brown sugar
1 bay leaf
2 cloves
½ – ¾ cup bread crumbs
dots of butter

1. Peel eggplant and dice into 1-inch squares. Boil in salt water for 12 minutes. Drain and place into greased baking dish.
2. In heavy saucepan melt butter, add flour and stir until well blended.
3. If using fresh tomatoes, peel and chop. Add tomatoes, pepper and onion to butter and flour mixture. Add salt, brown sugar, bay leaf and cloves. Cook 5 – 10 minutes.
4. Remove bay leaf and cloves. Pour mixture over eggplant in baking dish.
5. Cover with bread crumbs and dot with butter.
6. Bake at 350° for 30 minutes.

*—Ethel Stoner, John R. Stoner Vegetables*

# Eggplant Parmesan

*Makes 6 servings*

1 medium eggplant
1 Tbsp. cooking oil
1 cup bread crumbs
½ cup Parmesan cheese
2 Tbsp. parsley flakes
1 tsp. salt
1 tsp. oregano
6 small tomatoes, chopped

2 medium onions, chopped
1 green or red pepper,
   chopped
2 dashes garlic salt
2 Tbsp. oil
½ cup tomato sauce
1 cup cheddar cheese, grated

1. Peel eggplant, cut into ½-inch slices and brown lightly on both sides in cooking oil. Place into a 9″ × 13″ greased baking dish.
2. Mix bread crumbs, cheese, parsley, salt and oregano. Cover each eggplant slice with this mixture.
3. In a saucepan combine tomatoes, onions, peppers, garlic salt, oil and tomato sauce. Simmer 15 minutes and spread on top of eggplant in baking dish. Top with grated cheddar cheese.
4. Bake at 375° for 15 minutes.

*—Rose Meck, Robert S. Meck*

# Stuffed Acorn Squash

*Makes 4 servings*

2 acorn squash, halved and seeded
1 lb. ground beef or ground turkey
½ cup apple, chopped
1 tsp. curry powder
½ lb. cheese, cubed
2 Tbsp. marmalade or apricot preserves
1 cup apples, sliced thinly
1 Tbsp. margarine
¼ tsp. cinnamon
¼ tsp. nutmeg

1. Place squash in baking dish with cut side down. Bake at 400° for 35–40 minutes or until tender.
2. Brown meat and drain off excess fat. Add chopped apples and curry powder. Cook until tender. Add cheese and preserves, stirring occasionally until cheese is melted.
3. Sauté thin apple slices in margarine until tender. Season lightly with cinnamon and nutmeg.
4. Remove squash from oven, place on serving plates and fill cavity with meat mixture. Top with sautéed apples.

My family thinks this combination is out of this world!
— *Ethel Stoner, John R. Stoner Vegetables*

# Baked Squash

*Makes 6–8 servings*

2 cups summer squash, cubed
6 Tbsp. butter or margarine, melted
1 cup onion, chopped
1 cup cheese, grated
½ cup milk
½ cup cream
2 cups bread cubes

1. Mix all ingredients except bread cubes. Pour into greased casserole. Top with bread cubes.
2. Bake at 350° for 50 minutes. Reduce oven temperature to 300° and bake another 10 minutes.
— *Sara Jane Wenger, Tom's Flower Garden*

# Baked Zucchini Almondine

*Makes 6 servings*

4 cups zucchini, grated
1¼ cups cheese, grated
1 cup bread crumbs
¾ cup onion, chopped
¼ tsp. garlic powder
3 Tbsp. butter or margarine

1 tsp. salt
¼ tsp. pepper
½ cup milk
2 eggs
½ cup slivered almonds

1. Combine zucchini, 1 cup cheese and bread crumbs. Turn into greased 1½ -quart casserole dish and set aside.
2. Sauté onion and garlic powder in butter. Add salt and pepper and blend into zucchini.
3. Combine milk and eggs and pour over zucchini mixture, stirring to moisten.
4. Top with remaining cheese and almonds. Bake at 350° for 30 minutes.

Of all the ways to prepare zucchini, this is the best!
— *Ethel Stoner, John R. Stoner Vegetables*

# Baked Zucchini

*Makes 6 servings*

3 cups zucchini, sliced
1½ cups cracker crumbs
3 eggs, beaten
½ tsp. salt

½ cup butter, melted
2 cups cheddar cheese,
    shredded
1 cup milk

1. Mix all ingredients together and place in greased, uncovered casserole dish.
2. Bake at 350° for 45–55 minutes.

*Mrs. Ada Rohrer, John M. Markley Meats*

# Hot Herbed Tomatoes

*Makes 6 servings*

2 pints cherry tomatoes
¾ cup bread crumbs
⅓ cup onion, minced
¼ cup fresh parsley, minced
1 clove garlic, minced

¾ tsp. salt
¼ to ½ tsp. thyme
¼ tsp. pepper
¼ cup olive oil

1. Line baking dish with tomatoes (one layer). Bake at 375° for 10 minutes.
2. Mix all other ingredients except olive oil. Spread over tomatoes. Drizzle olive oil over top. Broil for 6–8 minutes until browned and heated through. Serve.

— *Sam Neff, S. Clyde Weaver, Inc.*

# Orange Beets

*Makes 4–6 servings*

2–3 medium beets, peeled
and grated
½ cup onion, chopped
2 Tbsp. butter or margarine,
melted
1 Tbsp. flour

3 Tbsp. orange juice
1 Tbsp. vinegar
3 Tbsp. brown sugar
¼ tsp. nutmeg

1. Cook beets in small amount of salt water until crispy tender (about 10–12 minutes).
2. Sauté onion in butter. Stir in flour, orange juice, vinegar and sugar. Cook, stirring constantly, until well blended.
3. Pour sauce over cooked beets. Season with nutmeg and serve.

— *Ethel Stoner, John R. Stoner Vegetables*

# Harvard Beets

*Makes 6 servings*

½ cup sugar
1½ tsp. cornstarch
¼ cup mild vinegar

¼ cup water
12 small cooked beets, sliced
2 Tbsp. butter

1. In a saucepan mix sugar and cornstarch. Add vinegar and water and bring to a boil. Boil 5 minutes.
2. Add sliced beets to mixture and turn off heat. Let stand for 30 minutes or longer. Just before serving, bring to a boil. Add butter and serve.

— *Mary K. Breighner, Rudolph Breighner*

# Cheese Scalloped Onions

*Makes 8 servings*

| | |
|---|---|
| 3 large onions, halved | 2 cups milk |
| 1 cup cheese, cubed | ½ tsp. salt |
| 4 slices buttered toast | ¼ tsp. pepper |
| ½ cup butter or margarine | 2 eggs, beaten |
| ½ cup flour | ½ cup bread crumbs |

1. Cook onions in boiling water about 10–15 minutes. Stir to separate into rings. Drain well and place half of onions into a 2-quart casserole. Add half of cheese and half of toast. Repeat the layers.
2. Melt butter, blend in flour and stir in milk gradually. Cook, stirring constantly, until thick. Add salt and pepper.
3. Add a little white sauce to the beaten eggs. Gradually add this mixture to rest of white sauce. Pour sauce over other layers. Top with bread crumbs.
4. Bake at 350° for 30 minutes.

—*Mrs. Ada Rohrer, John M. Markley Meats*

# Marinated Mushrooms

*Makes 4–6 servings*

| | |
|---|---|
| 1½ lbs. fresh mushrooms | 1 tsp. prepared mustard |
| ⅓ cup vinegar | 2 tsp. parsley flakes |
| ⅓ cup salad oil | 1 tsp. salt |
| 1 Tbsp. brown sugar | 1 small onion, thinly sliced |

1. Boil mushrooms 5 minutes and drain them.
2. Combine all other ingredients and pour over mushrooms. Chill in a covered dish overnight or at least several hours.

—*Rose Meck, Robert S. Meck*

My grandparents brought produce to the old curb market. They would get up at one o'clock in the morning and drive their horse-drawn market wagon from Mt. Nebo into the city of Lancaster. I remember how well-kept the market wagon was. They would park along the curb and sell produce from the wagon.

—*Miriam Hess, Frank Weaver Greenhouses*

# MEATS
## AND
# MEAT DISHES

# Chicken Provencal With Pesto

*Makes 6 – 8 servings*

**Chicken Ingredients:**
6 medium onions, coarsely chopped
½ cup olive oil
2 28-oz. cans plum tomatoes
1 Tbsp. fresh thyme or 1 tsp. dried thyme
1 Tbsp. fresh basil or 1 tsp. dried basil
1 Tbsp. fresh tarragon or 1 tsp. dried tarragon
1 Tbsp. fresh rosemary or 1 tsp. dried rosemary
4 cloves fresh garlic, minced
2 3-lb. chickens, cut up
2 cups chicken broth
4 cups dry white wine
1½ – 2 lbs. small new potatoes in skins
2 loaves French bread

**Pesto Ingredients:**
2 cups fresh basil or 2 Tbsp. dried basil
½ cup olive oil
2 Tbsp. pine nuts
2 cloves garlic, crushed
1 tsp. salt
½ cup Parmesan cheese, freshly grated
2 Tbsp. Romano cheese, grated
3 Tbsp. butter, softened

1. To prepare pesto blend all ingredients except cheeses and softened butter in a blender or food processor. Pour into a bowl and add cheeses and butter, mixing by hand.
2. In a skillet or Dutch oven sauté onions in olive oil until transparent. Add tomatoes with their juice. Add all herbs, garlic, chicken, broth, wine and half of pesto.
3. Cover and bake at 350° for 35 minutes. Add potatoes and bake 1 hour or until potatoes are tender when pierced with fork.
4. Serve in deep soup plates with plenty of hot French bread to mop up juices. Serve remaining pesto at table.

This is another peasant dish from Provence where cooking odors fill the house like perfume. Most of the dried herbs are available at my stand. Also available are the pine nuts for the all-time favorite pesto which is great year-round on pasta or in soups.
—*Regine Ibold, The Spice Stand*

# Chicken With 40 Cloves Garlic

*Makes 8 servings*

⅔ cup olive oil
8 chicken legs, 8 chicken thighs, with skin removed, if desired
4 ribs celery, chopped
2 medium onions, chopped
4 Tbsp. flat-leaf parsley, chopped
1 Tbsp. fresh tarragon or 1 tsp. dried
½ cup dry vermouth
salt and pepper to taste
nutmeg
40 cloves garlic, unpeeled
2 loaves French bread

1. Put olive oil in shallow dish and coat chicken pieces with it.
2. Cover bottom of a heavy 6-quart casserole with mixture of celery and onion. Add parsley and tarragon. Lay chicken pieces on top.
3. Pour vermouth over them. Sprinkle with salt, pepper and a little nutmeg. Intersperse garlic cloves with chicken pieces.
4. Cover tightly with foil and lid. Bake at 375° for 1½ hours without peeking.
5. Serve chicken pieces, pan juices and garlic cloves with thin slices of hot French bread. Garlic may be squeezed from its husk and spread on bread like butter.

I first prepared this Provencal dish 18 years ago, the night before my youngest son Hans was born. The next morning the nursery at St. Joseph's Hospital reeked of garlic! My doctor and pediatrician came to the room and said, "So this is the mother of the garlic baby!" They still call Hans "the garlic baby" and he is now 6′ 3″ and still loves garlic.

*— Regine Ibold, The Spice Stand*

My father, Edward Aaron Howry, first of a long line of Howry butchers to attend the market, operated a stand on the old curb market before he moved into the new Central Market house. As was the custom in those days, he dressed and sold meats only during the fall, winter and spring. During the summer months, he sold his strawberries and other fruits and vegetables.
—from the memories of the late Myrtle Howry Funk

# Hungarian Chicken Livers

*Makes 4 – 6 servings*

5 slices bacon
1 large green pepper,
  chopped
1 large onion, chopped
¾ lb. fresh mushrooms,
  cleaned and sliced

2 Tbsp. hot Hungarian
  paprika
1½ lbs. chicken livers
1 cup sour cream
cooked rice or noodles

1. Fry bacon in large skillet. Remove, crumble and reserve.
2. Pour all except ¼ cup bacon drippings from pan. Add chopped peppers and onions and sauté until golden. Add mushrooms and paprika and sauté a few minutes longer.
3. Rinse chicken livers. Pat dry. Add chicken livers to skillet and sauté over high heat until cooked through.
4. Remove from heat. Add bacon and sour cream. Return to burner and heat gently. Do not boil.
5. Serve over rice or noodles.

I love chicken livers and enjoy finding ways to dress them up.
— *Cindy Cover, Marion Cheese*

# Sour Cream Chicken

*Makes 8 servings*

1 cup sour cream
2 Tbsp. lemon juice
2 tsp. Worcestershire® sauce
1 tsp. paprika
1½ tsp. salt

¼ tsp. pepper
1 cup fine bread crumbs
½ cup margarine, melted
4 chicken breasts, split,
  boned and skinned

1. Combine all ingredients except bread crumbs, margarine and chicken breasts. Mix well.
2. Coat chicken breasts with this mixture and let stand overnight, covered.
3. Roll chicken in bread crumbs. Place chicken pieces in a baking dish. Spoon ¼ cup melted margarine over chicken. Bake uncovered at 325° for 40 minutes.
4. Spoon remaining margarine over chicken and bake 15 minutes longer.

Easy to prepare the day before an elegant dinner party!
— *Darla Lamoureux, Willow Valley Farms*

# One Dish Chicken and Gravy

*Makes 4 – 6 servings*

1 frying chicken, cut up
¼ cup flour
¼ cup butter, melted
1 tsp. onion, chopped
1 cup evaporated milk
1 can cream of mushroom
  soup

1 cup mild cheddar cheese,
  grated
¾ tsp. salt
⅛ tsp. pepper
paprika

1. Roll chicken in flour. Place skin down in melted butter in a
9″ × 13″ baking dish. Bake uncovered at 425° for 30 minutes.
Turn chicken and bake 10 – 15 minutes longer. Pour off excess fat.
2. In a separate bowl mix milk, soup, cheese, salt and pepper. Pour
over chicken and sprinkle with paprika. Cover with foil and bake at
325° for 20 minutes.
3. Serve with rice.

*— Helen Harnish, Willow Valley Farms*

# Chicken Crackers

*Makes 8 – 10 servings*

**Cracker Ingredients:**
2 cups flour
¾ cup butter
4 Tbsp. milk or cream
½ tsp. salt

**Chicken Ingredients:**
5 – 6 lb. whole chicken
1½ qts. chicken stock
chopped parsley

1. Cook chicken about 1 hour until tender. Remove meat from
bones and cut into pieces. Save chicken stock.
2. Prepare a gravy with chicken stock. Add chicken pieces and heat
thoroughly.
3. To prepare crackers mix ingredients as you would for pie
dough. Roll out thin. Cut into ¾″-squares and place on a greased
cookie sheet.
4. Bake at 425° for 10 minutes until golden brown.
5. Put crackers into one or two serving dishes and pour gravy over
top. Garnish with parsley and serve.

Grandmother Weaver served these along with ham, fish and
oyster crackers at a traditional Lancaster County family feed.

*— Mrs. S. Clyde Weaver, S. Clyde Weaver, Inc.*

**Variations:**
1. Use leftover turkey.
2. Freeze crackers and take out when ready to serve.

# Chicken Pot Pie With Puff Pastry

*Makes 4 – 6 servings*

1 large white cooking onion
2 ribs celery, chopped
4 Tbsp. butter or margarine
3 large carrots, cut on bias
2 cups peas
1 cup green beans

1 quart chicken stock
1½ lbs. chicken tenderloin
4 Tbsp. flour plus ½ cup
  water
1 lb. piece puff pastry

1. Sauté onion and celery in butter or margarine. Set aside.
2. Blanch carrots, peas and green beans for 4 minutes. Set aside.
3. Bring chicken stock to a boil.
4. Poach chicken in stock until just done, about 5 minutes. Remove chicken. Cut into bite-sized pieces.
5. In separate bowl whisk flour and water until smooth. Add slowly to chicken stock, whisking until smooth. Add all other ingredients, including chicken, to stock.
6. Spoon into a 9″ × 12″ greased baking dish.
7. Top with a piece of puff pastry. Trim so pastry just covers the edge. Bake at 350° for 40 minutes. When finished, pastry will be golden brown.

Country favorite with an elegant touch!
—*Kathleen Pianka, Marion Cheese*

# Susquehanna Riverman's Pot Pie

*Makes 8 servings*

4½ – 5 lb. stewing hen
1 cup eggs
½ tsp. salt

1 Tbsp. lard or chicken fat
½ cup mashed potatoes
3 cups flour

1. Cook stewing hen until tender. Pick the meat off the bones and cut meat into bite-size pieces. Save broth for pot pie.
2. Beat eggs slightly with fork. Add salt, lard and mashed potatoes (warm or cold). Work in as much flour as needed to make an easy rolling dough. Roll thin and cut into 2-inch squares. Drop piece by piece into briskly boiling broth.
Grandmother's tip: Add meat when pot pie is almost done. Overcooking of the cut-up meat causes it to separate and become stringy.

This recipe follows the Pensylvania Dutch phrases and words as handed down by grandmothers and great-grandmothers. A slight variation of this recipe is used for pot pie suppers at the Quarryville, Pennsylvania Community Fair.
—*Helen McComsey Rohrer, McComsey Family*

# Plantain and Chicken Curry

*Makes 4 servings*

1 ripe plantain (yellow skin with black spots), cubed
4 chicken breasts
1 onion, sliced
1 medium apple, peeled and cut in cubes
4 Tbsp. butter
1 bay leaf
2 Tbsp. coconut flakes
3 tsp. curry powder
3 Tbsp. flour
salt and pepper to taste
½ pint heavy cream

1. Boil chicken breasts until tender in about 4 cups water. Remove chicken from broth; reserve 1½ cups broth. Cut chicken in bite-size cubes.
2. In a saucepan sauté onion and apple in butter. Add bay leaf, coconut flakes and curry powder. Sprinkle with flour and sauté for 3 minutes. While stirring, add reserved broth.
3. When sauce is smooth, add salt and pepper to taste. Add cream, plantain and chicken. Simmer for 10 minutes.
4. Serve over bed of rice and garnish with coconut flakes.

— *Betty Lichty, Horn of Plenty*

# Turkey Filling

*Makes 10–12 servings*

1 small turkey or 1 large roasting chicken
4 cups soft bread crumbs
2 eggs
2 tsp. salt
1 cup celery, finely chopped
1 cup carrots, finely chopped
1 can cream of mushroom soup
1 cup milk

1. Roast turkey or chicken in oven until very soft. Reserve the breast for cold sandwiches.
2. Remove all meat from bones. Put all ingredients into large mixing bowl, including broth from baking the fowl. Mix well adding milk as needed. This mixture should be very moist.
3. Put into roaster and bake at 350° for 30 minutes to 1 hour.

— *Mary W. Hess, Funk Brothers, Inc.*

# Turkey Loaf

*Makes 8 servings*

| | |
|---|---|
| 3 eggs | 1 tsp. salt |
| 1½ cups tomato juice | pepper to taste |
| 1 cup quick oats | 3 lbs. ground turkey |
| 1 tsp. Worcestershire® sauce | 2 – 3 Tbsp. ketchup |
| 1 tsp. poultry seasoning | |

1. Beat eggs. Add tomato juice, oats, Worcestershire® sauce, poultry seasoning, salt and pepper. Blend well. Add ground turkey and mix well.
2. Form into a loaf and place in a greased 9″ × 13″ pan. Brush top with ketchup.
3. Bake at 350° for 1 – 1¼ hours.

I like this recipe because it is low in cholesterol.
— *Ruth L. Mellinger, C. H. Thomas and Son*

# Shepherd's Pie

*Makes 4 servings*

| | |
|---|---|
| 2 cups mashed potatoes | 1 cup gravy |
| 2 cups cooked vegetables | ¼ tsp. pepper |
| 1 cup turkey, cooked and diced | ¼ tsp. oregano |
| | ¼ tsp. basil |
| 3 slices bread, cubed | dash of seasoning salt |

1. Line a greased baking dish with 1 cup mashed potatoes.
2. Fill with vegetables, turkey (or any leftover meat), bread cubes, gravy and seasonings. Cover with 1 cup mashed potatoes.
3. Bake at 350° for 30 – 40 minutes.

Great way to use leftovers!
— *Denise Torbert, The Goodie Shoppe*

Mother always made me stay close by her stand. I was not permitted to run around the market. I would take naps under the stand while Mother waited on customers.
— *Viv Hunt, Viv's Varieties*

# Glazed Ham Balls

*Makes 8 – 10 servings*

**Ham Ingredients:**
2½ lbs. cooked ground ham
1¼ cups uncooked oatmeal
1 cup milk
3 eggs, slightly beaten

**Sauce Ingredients:**
1 cup plus 2 Tbsp. light
   brown sugar, firmly
   packed
3 Tbsp. cornstarch
1½ Tbsp. prepared mustard
1¾ cups pineapple juice
½ cup light corn syrup
3 Tbsp. cider vinegar
½ tsp. cloves

1. Combine ham, oatmeal, milk and eggs. Shape into 1½ inch balls (makes about 40 – 45 balls). Place in a lightly greased baking dish.
2. Combine all ingredients for sauce. Bring to a boil, stirring constantly. Reduce heat and simmer for 3 minutes. Pour sauce over ham balls. Bake at 350° for 1 hour.

Sometimes I serve these for Sunday dinner when we are the host family for church.

—*Arlene Leaman, S. Clyde Weaver, Inc.*

# Weaver's Ham Loaf

*Makes 4 – 6 servings*

**Ham Ingredients:**
1 lb. Weaver's fresh, bulk
   sausage
1 lb. ground ham
2 eggs
1 cup bread crumbs
1 cup milk
1 tsp. prepared mustard

**Syrup Ingredients:**
½ cup water
½ cup cider vinegar
½ cup brown sugar
1 tsp. dry mustard

1. Mix thoroughly all ingredients for ham and form into small individual loaves. Bake at 350° for 45 minutes.
2. While ham bakes, prepare syrup by mixing all ingredients and bring to a boil, stirring constantly.
3. Baste ham loaves with syrup and continue baking for another 30 minutes.

This recipe was developed by my mother and often served to company.

—*Arlene Leaman, S. Clyde Weaver, Inc.*

◆

# Apricot Ham Glaze With Mustard Sauce

*Makes 12 – 16 servings*

*Ham Ingredients:*
8 – 10 lb. ham
½ cup apricot jam
2 Tbsp. cider vinegar
2 Tbsp. Dijon® mustard
cloves

*Mustard Sauce Ingredients:*
½ cup Dijon® mustard
6 – 8 Tbsp. maple syrup

1. Score ham. Dot with cloves.
2. Mix jam, vinegar and 2 Tbsp. mustard together.
3. With the fattier side up spread ½ of jam mixture over top of ham. Bake at 325° for 1½ hours.
4. Reglaze and bake an additional 1 hour.
5. Reglaze and bake an additional ½ hour.
6. To prepare mustard sauce mix maple syrup with ½ cup mustard. Serve with baked ham.

— *Sam and Nancy Neff, S. Clyde Weaver, Inc.*

**Variation:**
Use peach jam instead of apricot jam.

# Elegant Creamed Ham

*Makes 4 – 6 servings*

½ cup butter or margarine
½ cup onion, diced
1 cup celery, diced
1 cup red or green pepper, diced
½ cup plus 2 Tbsp. flour

½ tsp. dry mustard
1 tsp. Worcestershire® sauce
½ tsp. Tabasco® sauce
5 cups milk
1 cup cheddar cheese, grated
1 lb. cooked ham, chopped

1. Melt butter in large pan. Add onion, celery and peppers. Cook until onion is yellow. Over low heat blend flour and seasonings into mixture. Gradually stir in milk. Cook until thickened, stirring constantly.
2. Add cheese and ham and heat thoroughly.
3. Serve over biscuits, toasted English muffins, waffles or toast.

Easy to prepare, great for a quick meal or even a midnight treat.

— *Ruth S. Landis, Kiefer's Meats and Cheese*

# Pineapple Glaze

*Makes 1½ cups*

**1 cup pineapple juice**
**1 Tbsp. cornstarch**
**⅓ cup light corn syrup**
**¼ cup light brown sugar, firmly packed**

1. In a saucepan mix pineapple juice and cornstarch. Stir until smooth.
2. Add all remaining ingredients and bring to a boil over medium heat, stirring constantly.

Delicious over ham! Leftover glaze tastes wonderful over ice cream.

*—Frances Kiefer, Kiefer's Meats and Cheese*

# Roasted Pig Stomach

*Makes 8 – 10 servings*

**1 pig stomach**
**1 small onion, chopped**
**½ cup celery, chopped**
**2 Tbsp. butter**
**2 eggs**
**4 – 6 cups bread, cubed**

**1 quart potatoes, diced**
**1½ lbs. ground sausage**
**milk or water to moisten bread**
**salt and pepper to taste**

1. Sauté onion and celery in butter.
2. Mix eggs and bread cubes. Add onions and celery. Add potatoes and sausage. Add enough liquid (milk or water) to moisten the mixture. Mix thoroughly. Season to taste.
3. Stuff the pig stomach with sausage filling, being careful not to fill too tightly since the stomach shrinks while baking. Close opening of stomach with thread or skewer.
4. Place stuffed stomach in a roasting pan with ½ cup water and bake covered at 350° for 2 hours. Uncover and bake another hour or until skin is brown and tender.
5. If you have more sausage filling than you need, bake the rest of it in a casserole.

The Leaman family has warm memories of the days when Grandma would have the whole family (about 30 people) over for a Sunday dinner of roasted pig stomach!

*—Arlene Leaman, S. Clyde Weaver, Inc.*

*The North American*, Philadelphia, Sunday, July 5, 1908

# HOW IS THIS FOR A HOUSEWIFE'S PARADISE?

*If there is a paradise for the market goer, it should be Lancaster. The fame of the fair city and its wonderful markets has spread beyond the borders of the state. Many Philadelphians go there to purchase supplies for their tables.*

*Fresh and delicious from the surrounding country, these supplies come every market day, and the prices prevailing are astonishingly cheap, when compared with these of larger cities. Market Day in Lancaster is an institution, and one of which the pretty city is justly proud. And its busy scenes are full of interest for the chance visitor.*

---

Beginning about 1 o'clock every market morning, miscellaneous processions of vehicles from various directions clatter and rumble into Lancaster.

Entering the city, the wagons pass down tree embowered streets, glimmering with the fitful blue luster of electric lamps. Closed shutters frown down upon the picturesque drivers of the wagons—men with patriarchal beards and broad-brimmed hats and women huddled up on the seats wearing plain dresses with peaked capes and plain bonnets.

To various hotels in the city they drive the wagons. They go into the rear sheds of the Farmer's Hotel, the Franklin House, the Sorrel Horse, the Lincoln and the Leopard. While a man climbs out and ties the horse a woman jumps from the wagon, several young girls, even children, appear mysteriously, rubbing their eyes. A lantern is lit and they begin unloading the wagon—a wagon bursting with fatness—of baskets of vegetables, eggs, butter, meat, chickens and a plethora of things good to eat.

By the time the sun rises, more than 1500 farmers will have arrived, and by 10 o'clock possibly from 10,000 to 12,000 people will have purchased their eatables. Considering the size of the city, it is possibly the biggest market in the United States, and, many claim, the cheapest.

At 2 o'clock Saturday morning the doors of the Central Market House are opened; at 3 the buyers begin to arrive. At the other markets people go still earlier. By 9 or 10 the markets are over.

"The people who don't want to get up in the morning," declared a citizen, "go to the afternoon market." This market, however, is largely attended by the families of working men who get paid Saturday morning.

Saturday is the big market day. From outlying towns, people come on trolley cars with great big baskets. From towns five, 10 and 15 miles away, thrifty housewives come; even from Philadelphia many come on Saturdays with great hampers, to [gather] in the week's supply of vegetables. Scores of families of railroad employees living in Philadelphia who enjoy annual passes do their marketing in Lancaster.

From 4 o'clock in the morning—before the sun illumines the narrow streets about it—until after 9 o'clock, crowds throng the market house. From 500 to 1000 persons flow in a steady stream along the aisles between the stalls at times.

Most of them are women, with big baskets holding a bushel of stuff. Some evidently are poor, with cheap dresses; others very elegantly attired.

Mayor J.P. McCaskey naturally regards Lancaster with pride.

"There is no doubt the markets are about the finest and cheapest in the country," he declared. "The people of the country get their wealth from the soil—they don't depend upon Wall Street."

# Chafing Dish Meat Balls

*Makes 6 – 8 servings*

2 lb. ground beef
1 egg, slightly beaten
1 large onion, grated
salt and pepper to taste

12-oz. bottle chili sauce
10-oz. jar grape jelly
juice of 1 lemon

1. Thoroughly mix ground beef, egg and onion. Salt and pepper to taste. Shape into small balls.
2. Mix chili sauce, grape jelly and lemon juice. Drop meat balls into sauce in a pan. Simmer until meat balls are brown.
3. Serve in a chafing dish.

If you prepare this recipe ahead of time and freeze it, it is an easy dish to serve anytime.

— *Viv Hunt, Viv's Varieties*

# Porcupine Balls

*Makes 4 – 6 servings*

1 cup bread crumbs
1 cup milk
2 eggs, beaten
1 lb. hamburger
1 medium onion, chopped

½ cup celery, chopped
(optional)
¼ cup rice, uncooked
2 cups tomato juice

1. Soak bread crumbs in milk. Add beaten eggs. Add all other ingredients except tomato juice and mix well. Shape into balls.
2. Place balls into baking dish. Pour tomato juice over balls and bake at 350° for 1½ hours.

— *Willow Valley Farms*

# Meat Loaf

*Makes 6 – 8 servings*

2 lbs. hamburger
2 eggs
1½ cups bread crumbs

1 pkg. onion soup mix
¾ cup ketchup
8-oz. can tomato sauce

1. Mix all ingredients except tomato sauce.
2. Shape into loaf and put into loaf pan. Pour tomato sauce over top.
3. Bake at 375° for 1 hour.

— *Esther Eisenberger, Eisenberger's Baked Goods*

◆

# Koenigsberger Klopse
# (delicate croquettes in sauce)

*Makes 4 – 5 servings*

*Klopse Ingredients:*
9 slices stale white bread, crusts removed
5 anchovy fillets
1¾ lbs. ground meat, mixture of beef and pork
2 cups potatoes, cooked and grated
2 eggs
1 Tbsp. flour
⅜ tsp. salt
dash of pepper
2 Tbsp. capers
flour

*Sauce Ingredients:*
3 Tbsp. butter, rounded
2 Tbsp. flour, rounded
3 Tbsp. capers
1½ tsp. lemon juice
½ tsp. salt, rounded
pepper
4 cups soup stock

1. Soak bread in water about 2 minutes. Squeeze water out of bread.
2. Mince anchovies as fine as possible. Blend bread, anchovies, ground meat, potatoes, eggs, flour, salt, pepper and capers together well.
3. Form mixture into 18 balls about the size of small eggs. Roll balls in flour and drop into a large deep pot of boiling salted water. Cook for 12 minutes. Remove from water and keep klopse warm.
4. To prepare sauce melt butter in a large kettle with a lid. Add flour and blend well with a fork. Do not brown. Add capers, lemon juice, salt and pepper.
5. Bring soup stock to a boil in a separate pan. Add boiling soup stock to sauce. Stir well with a fork or egg whisk to prevent lumps. Cover and simmer slowly for 15 minutes, stirring frequently to prevent burning.
6. Add klopse to sauce and simmer for 5 minutes.
7. Serve with mashed potatoes and asparagus.

*—Christine Weiss, German Deli*

# Barbecued Beef Patties

*Makes about 8 patties*

**Meat Ingredients:**
1 lb. ground beef
1 cup bread crumbs
½ cup milk
2 eggs
1 tsp. salt
⅛ tsp. pepper

**Sauce Ingredients:**
1½ Tbsp. Worcestershire®
   sauce
3 Tbsp. brown sugar
¼ cup vinegar
½ cup ketchup
½ cup water
½ cup onions, chopped

1. Mix all meat ingredients well. Shape into patties or balls. Place into a long, greased baking dish.
2. Mix all sauce ingredients well. Pour sauce over patties.
3. Bake uncovered at 350° for 1 hour.

When I was little, it was always special when Mother made these meat balls.

—*Judith E. Martin, Paul L. Sensenig and Sons*

# Salisbury Steak

*Makes 6 servings*

**Steak Ingredients:**
2 lbs. ground beef
2 tsp. salt
⅛ tsp. pepper
1 egg, well beaten
¼ cup onion, chopped

6 crackers, broken
½ cup milk
1 tsp. parsley
⅛ tsp. oregano
⅛ tsp. basil

**Gravy Ingredients:**
3 cups water
2 Tbsp. flour

1 cup water
salt and pepper to taste

1. Soak crackers in milk.
2. Mix together all ingredients for beef patties. Shape mixture into 6 oblong patties and brown slightly on each side. Save the drippings. Place into a baking dish.
3. Prepare a gravy by adding 3 cups water to the beef drippings. Bring to a boil. Make a smooth paste with flour and 1 cup water. Add paste to boiling drippings in a thin stream. Stir quickly and constantly to prevent lumps. Add seasonings. Heat until thickened. Pour gravy over beef patties.
4. Bake at 300° for 45 minutes.

—*Janice Kreider, Eisenberger's Baked Goods*

◆

# Creamed Dried Beef

*Makes 3 – 4 servings*

**1 – 2 Tbsp. butter**
**¼ lb. chipped dried beef**
**4 Tbsp. flour**
**3 cups milk**

1. Melt butter in skillet over low heat. Add dried beef and stir occasionally until lightly browned.
2. Add flour. Stir until dried beef is well coated with flour. Slowly add milk, stirring constantly. Stir until thickened.
3. Serve over toast.

Quick and easy!

*— Ruth Martin, C. Z. Martin Sons*

**Variation:**
Use chipped turkey ham instead of dried beef.

# Roast Beef

*Makes 10 – 12 servings*

**3 – 4 lb. beef roast or round steak**
**1 can cream of mushroom soup**
**1 pkg. dry onion soup mix**
**salt and pepper to taste**

1. Fit a large piece of foil into a pan large enough to hold the meat. Place meat onto foil and fold foil up to hold the liquid.
2. Pour mushroom soup and dry onion soup over meat. Salt and pepper to taste. Fold foil tightly over meat, sealing it well.
3. Roast slowly at 300° for 3 hours or until meat is finished to one's taste.

This is delicious and the gravy is ready to serve!
*— Jean Risser, Hoffmaster and Wike, The Wooden Carrousel*

## Savory Sweet Pot Roast

*Makes 6 – 8 servings*

3 – 4 lb. boneless beef roast
1 medium onion, sliced
1 can cream of mushroom
 soup
½ cup water

¾ cup brown sugar
¼ cup vinegar
2 tsp. salt
1 tsp. mustard
1 tsp. Worcestershire® sauce

1. Brown meat on both sides. Add onions.
2. Blend together all other ingredients and pour over meat. Cover and simmer for 2½ to 3 hours.

—*Mildred Brackbill, Utz's Potato Chips*

## Sweet and Sour Brisket

*Makes 10 servings*

6 lb. beef brisket
2 onions, sliced
¾ cup brown sugar
½ cup vinegar

1 cup ketchup
1 cup water
1 Tbsp. salt
pepper

1. Place brisket in a heavy saucepan. Brown on all sides. Add onions and brown them.
2. Blend all other ingredients and pour over meat. Cover and simmer for 3 hours.

This recipe was given to me by a favorite cousin. I enjoy serving it to guests.

—*Ruth Eshleman, Givant's Bakery*

C. H. Thomas and Sons is in its third generation on Central Market. I loved coming to market with my grandfather Elmer Thomas when I was a young boy. My father operated the stand in those days and he normally left for market around 2 a.m. We boys would wait until later and ride in with our grandfather.

—*Ernie Thomas, C. H. Thomas and Sons*

◆

# Grilled Leg of Lamb

*Makes 8 servings*

**5–6 lb. leg of lamb, boned and butterflied**

| *Marinade Ingredients:* | *Final Basting Ingredients:* |
|---|---|
| ¼ cup olive oil | ¼ cup lemon juice |
| 1 Tbsp. oregano | ½ tsp. oregano |
| 1 tsp. rosemary | 1 tsp. salt |
| 1 tsp. thyme | |
| ¼ tsp. black pepper | |

1. Mix all ingredients for oil marinade. Place butterflied leg in baking dish and pour marinade over top. Marinate 2 hours, turning occasionally.
2. Place leg on charcoal grill (gas grill tends to flame and needs water to control).
3. Use marinade oil to baste leg as it cooks, turning occasionally. Salt as you prefer.
4. Grill until thermometer registers 140° in thickest meat portion.
5. Mix final basting ingredients and use to baste leg. Continue grilling until thermometer registers 160° for pink and 175° for well done.
6. Serve with lemon wedges.

The lemon is used to cut the fat of the lamb. If you have ever been offended by the "wooliness" of lamb/mutton, this recipe is worth a try. The lemon makes a lot of difference. Do not use lemon baste too early in grilling process or it will dry out the meat.
— *Sam Neff, S. Clyde Weaver, Inc.*

# Lamb Stew

*Makes 8 servings*

| | |
|---|---|
| 1 Tbsp. olive oil | 2 Tbsp. fruit jelly |
| 3 cups roast lamb cubes | 2 Tbsp. tomato paste or 4–6 |
| ½ cup brandy or cognac | Tbsp. tomato sauce |
| ¼ cup wine vinegar | 1 tsp. dry rosemary |
| 1 cup dry red wine | 1 tsp. thyme |
| 2 cups beef stock | 1 tsp. black pepper |
| 12 pearl onions | 2 bay leaves |
| 4 carrots, chopped | ¼ cup parsley, chopped |
| 2–3 potatoes, chopped | ½–1 tsp. salt |
| 2 Tbsp. corn or potato starch | |

1. Heat olive oil in skillet and brown lamb cubes. Transfer to casserole dish.

2. Heat brandy or cognac in skillet and ignite. Add vinegar, wine and beef stock. Bring to a boil. Add all remaining ingredients and cook 5–10 minutes. Pour mixture into casserole with lamb cubes and stir gently.

3. Cover and bake at 350° for 1 hour. Uncover and bake another 30 minutes. Serve.

This is an excellent way to use leftover roast lamb. I have tried it with fresh lamb and find it is just not the same.

*— Sam Neff, S. Clyde Weaver, Inc.*

# Lamb Balls With Sour Cream and Capers

*Makes 4 – 6 servings*

**Meat Ingredients:**
1½ lb. ground lamb
½ cup onion, chopped
1 clove garlic, minced
½ cup bread crumbs
1 egg, beaten
2 Tbsp. parsley
2 Tbsp. dill
¼ tsp. thyme
½ tsp. lemon juice

**Sauce Ingredients:**
1½ Tbsp. butter or margarine
½ cup onion, chopped
1 Tbsp. paprika
½ tsp. dried thyme
½ cup white wine
1 cup chicken broth
2 Tbsp. cornstarch dissolved in 2 Tbsp. water
3 Tbsp. capers, drained
1 cup sour cream
2 Tbsp. chopped dill
salt and pepper to taste

1. Mix all meat ingredients and roll into balls. Sauté meat balls until lightly browned. Remove from pan. Pour off excess fat.

2. To prepare sauce sauté onion in 1½ Tbsp. butter or margarine and add paprika, thyme and wine. Bring mixture to a boil and add chicken broth. Bring to boil again and thicken slightly with cornstarch and water mixture.

3. Add meat balls, capers, sour cream, dill, salt and pepper. Heat, but do NOT bring to a boil.

4. Serve over rice or barley.

Before returning to the family business, Nancy and I lived in Crete for two years. This is an adaptation of a recipe from that area. It tastes great and does not have any of the gaminess some people associate with lamb.

*— Sam Neff, S. Clyde Weaver, Inc.*

# Haddock Flake Pie

*Makes 6 servings*

3 Tbsp. butter
1 onion, sliced
3 Tbsp. flour
1 tsp. salt
⅛ tsp. pepper
⅛ tsp. thyme
½ cup rich milk
1½ cups fish stock

2 small carrots, cooked and diced
1 small potato, cooked and diced
1 tsp. Worcestershire® sauce
1 lb. haddock, flaked
1 8″ unbaked pie dough topping

1. Melt butter and brown onion lightly. Stir in flour, salt, pepper and thyme. When well blended add milk and fish stock, stirring constantly.
2. Continue stirring and add potatoes and carrots. Stir until sauce thickens. Add Worcestershire® sauce and fish flakes. Pour into a casserole dish and cover with pastry crust.
3. Bake at 450° for 20–25 minutes or until top is golden brown.
    —*Charles Fox and Larry McElhenny, New Holland Seafood*

# Deviled Crab Meat

*Makes 6 servings*

2 Tbsp. butter
2½ Tbsp. flour
1½ cups milk
2 cups crab meat

1 tsp. salt
¼ tsp. paprika
2 Tbsp. lemon juice
1 cup buttered bread crumbs

1. Melt butter and add flour. Slowly stir in milk to make a white sauce.
2. Mix crab meat, salt, paprika and lemon juice and add to white sauce, stirring constantly.
3. Pour mixture into a buttered casserole and put bread crumbs on top. Bake at 400° for 25 minutes.

This receipt came from my aunt in Norfolk, VA. She was known for her seafood dinners.

    —*Ruth Eshleman, Givant's Bakery*

# Cheesy Crab Pie

*Makes one 9-inch pie*

| | |
|---|---|
| ½ cup mayonnaise | 6½ oz. can flaked crab meat |
| 2 Tbsp. flour | 8 ozs. Swiss cheese, grated |
| 2 eggs, beaten | ⅓ cup onion, chopped |
| 1 cup evaporated milk | 1 9″ unbaked pie shell |

1. Combine mayonnaise, flour, eggs and milk. Mix until well blended.
2. Drain crab meat and grate cheese. Add crab meat, cheese and onion to mayonnaise mixture.
3. Place into unbaked pie shell and bake at 350° for 40–45 minutes.

*—Ethel Stoner, John R. Stoner Vegetables*

**Variations:**
   1. Add green peppers.
   2. Use Italian Fontina cheese instead of Swiss. It does not become rubbery when cooked and allows the crab to show better.

# Crab Cakes

*Makes 10–12 servings*

**Crab Meat Ingredients:**
1 lb. crab meat
2 Tbsp. lemon juice
2 eggs
2 Tbsp. mayonnaise
1 cup bread crumbs
⅛ tsp. pepper
1 tsp. dry mustard
1 tsp. Worcestershire® sauce

**White Sauce Ingredients:**
1 Tbsp. butter
1 Tbsp. all-purpose flour
½ cup milk
salt to taste

**Breading Ingredients:**
3 Tbsp. flour
½ cup bread crumbs
2–3 Tbsp. shortening

1. Pick over crab meat and discard any bits of shell or cartilage. Sprinkle lemon juice over crab meat.
2. Make a medium white sauce by melting butter, flour, milk and salt to taste. Stir constantly until mixture is smooth and thick.
3. Beat eggs, then mix them with the white sauce, mayonnaise, bread crumbs and seasonings. Stir well. Gently combine crab meat with mixture. Chill until firm enough to shape into cakes.
4. Prepare crumbs for breading cakes by mixing 3 Tbsp. flour and ½ cup bread crumbs.
5. Bread crab cakes and fry in shortening, turning a few times, until both sides are browned.

My favorite seafood recipe. Delicious with a baked potato and salad.

*—Ruth Widders, Irwin S. Widders Produce*

# Scallops and Pasta Romano

*Makes 6 servings*

1 lb. bay scallops
2 cloves garlic, minced
¼ cup butter or margarine
¼ cup butter or margarine,
    softened
2 Tbsp. dried parsley flakes
1 tsp. dried basil
¼ tsp. pepper

8-oz. pkg. cream cheese,
    softened
⅔ cup boiling water
8 ozs. fettucini, linguine or
    spaghetti
¾ cup Romano or Parmesan
    cheese, grated

1. Cook scallops and garlic in ¼ cup butter or margarine which has not been softened until scallops are done. Keep warm.
2. Combine softened butter or margarine, parsley and basil. Blend in pepper and cream cheese. Stir in boiling water and mix well. Keep warm over pan of hot water.
3. Cook pasta according to package directions and drain.
4. Toss scallop mixture into pasta. Sprinkle with ½ cup grated cheese and toss.
5. Pour cream cheese mixture over pasta and toss until well coated. Place pasta into serving dish and sprinkle with remaining ¼ cup grated cheese.

Wonderful combination of seafood, pasta and spices!
— *Cynthia Strube, Marion Cheese*

# Shrimp or Roast Pork Fried Rice

*Makes 4 servings*

4 Tbsp. oil
2 eggs
pinch of salt
1 clove garlic, minced
4 cups cooked rice
¼ tsp. sugar

2 Tbsp. soy sauce
1 cup roast pork or cooked
    shrimp, diced
½ cup sliced carrots, cooked
½ cup peas, cooked

1. Beat eggs lightly and add a pinch of salt. Heat 1 Tbsp. oil in a frying pan and scramble eggs until they are cooked through but still moist and fluffy. Remove from pan and cut into small pieces.
2. Scrape pan and heat the remaining 3 Tbsp. oil. Add minced garlic and rice and stir-fry 3–4 minutes until coated with oil.
3. Dissolve sugar in soy sauce and sprinkle mixture over rice. Add the eggs and roast pork or shrimp. Stir until well mixed.
4. Add carrots and peas and heat through before serving.
— *Tuyen Kim Ho, Kim's Candies*

# Cajun Shrimp

*Makes 3 large servings*

1 lb. shrimp
¼ tsp. ground cayenne
  pepper
¼ tsp. black pepper
½ tsp. salt
½ tsp. crushed red pepper
½ tsp. dried thyme leaves
1 tsp. dried basil leaves

½ tsp. dried oregano leaves
⅓ cup margarine
3 cloves garlic, minced
1 tsp. Worcestershire® sauce
2 cups tomatoes, diced
¼ cup beer, room
  temperature

1. Peel and de-vein shrimp under cold running water. Drain well.
2. Combine all dry seasonings. In a large skillet or wok, combine margarine, garlic, Worcestershire® sauce and dry seasonings. Stir over high heat until margarine is melted.
3. Add the tomatoes and the shrimp. Cook for approximately 3 minutes (until shrimp is almost cooked), stirring constantly.
4. Add the beer. Cover and cook for 1 minute longer. Serve over rice with crusty French bread.

Great to serve to friends, but be sure the friends enjoy hot and spicy food!

— *Cynthia Strube, Marion Cheese*

# Poached Salmon

*Makes 4 servings*

*Meat Ingredients:*
4 salmon steaks, 1″ thick,
  skinned
½ cup white wine
½ cup water
dill sprigs
1 lemon, sliced

*Sauce Ingredients:*
1 cup mayonnaise
1 cup crème fraiche
2 Tbsp. lemon juice
1 tsp. white wine
½ tsp. salt
½ tsp. white pepper
3 Tbsp. fresh dill
dash of cayenne pepper

1. Poach salmon steaks in ½ cup wine and ½ cup water for 15 minutes.
2. Prepare a dill sauce by combining mayonnaise, crème fraiche, lemon juice, white wine, salt, pepper, dill and cayenne pepper.
3. Let salmon cool to room temperature and cover with dill sauce. Garnish with lemon slices and dill sprigs. Serve.

Cool, refreshing dish for summer entertaining!
— *Pam Griffe, The Goodie Shoppe*

◆

# Baked Salmon

*Makes 4 servings*

**2 cups salmon, broken into pieces**
**2 cups cracker crumbs**
**2 eggs, beaten**
**2 cups hot milk**
**butter and salt to taste**

1. Put alternate layers of salmon and cracker crumbs into a greased baking dish.
2. Beat eggs and slowly add hot milk. Pour over salmon and crumbs. Add butter and salt.
3. Bake at 375° for 40 minutes.
   —*Jean Risser, Hoffmaster and Wike, The Wooden Carrousel*

# Stuffed Flounder in Creamed Basil Sauce

*Makes 6 – 8 servings*

**¼ cup onion, chopped**
**4 Tbsp. butter or margarine**
**½ lb. fresh crab meat or**
   **7½-oz. can crab meat**
**½ cup fresh mushrooms or**
   **3-oz. can mushrooms,**
   **drained**
**½ cup cracker crumbs**
**2 Tbsp. parsley**
**2 Tbsp. mayonnaise**
**2 lbs. flounder fillets (8)**

**3 Tbsp. flour**
**1 cup milk**
**3-oz. pkg. cream cheese,**
   **softened**
**1 Tbsp. basil**
**garlic powder**
**1 Tbsp. Worcestershire®**
   **sauce**
**4 ozs. Swiss cheese, grated**
**paprika**

1. Sauté onion in 1 Tbsp. butter until onion is transparent. Stir in crab meat, mushrooms, cracker crumbs, parsley and mayonnaise. Spread mixture over fillets.
2. Roll up fillets and place seam side down in greased baking dish.
3. Melt remaining 3 Tbsp. butter in saucepan. Blend in flour and add milk, cream cheese and mushroom liquid (if desired). Cook mixture until it thickens. Add basil, garlic powder and Worcestershire® sauce.
4. Pour mixture over fillets in baking dish. Bake at 400° for 25 minutes. Remove from oven and sprinkle with Swiss cheese and paprika. Return to oven and bake 10 minutes longer.
   —*Ethel Stoner, John R. Stoner Vegetables*

# CASSEROLES

# Company Stew

*Makes 4 servings*

| | |
|---|---|
| 2 thick slices slab bacon | 1 large onion |
| 1½ lb. chuck roast | 2 large tomatoes |
| 1 cup flour | 1 lb. miniature new potatoes |
| salt and pepper to taste | 1 tsp. nutmeg |
| 2 large cloves garlic | 1½ tsp. thyme |
| 1 cup dry red wine | 1 Tbsp. parsley |
| 1 cup beef broth or beef bouillon | |

1. Cut bacon into pieces and cook in small roaster or Dutch oven.
2. Cut beef into bite-size pieces. Salt and pepper and dredge in flour. Remove bacon pieces from roaster. Add beef to bacon drippings and brown. Add garlic. Add wine, stirring to loosen any bits from bottom of roaster.
3. Chop onion and tomatoes. Add all remaining ingredients to roaster. Return bacon pieces to roaster and stir mixture thoroughly.
4. Cover and bake at 325° for 2½ hours. After 1½ hours, taste. Adjust salt and pepper to taste.

Served with crusty bread and green salad, this hearty, flavorful stew is great for cold winter evenings or tailgate parties.

— *Cynthia Strube, Marion Cheese*

# Beef Stew

*Makes 8 servings*

| | |
|---|---|
| 2 lbs. beef cubes | 1 Tbsp. salt |
| 2 cups carrots, diced | ½ tsp. pepper |
| 2 cups potatoes, diced | 1 cup tomato juice |
| 2 medium onions, sliced | 1 cup water |
| 1 cup celery, chopped | 1 Tbsp. brown sugar |
| 2 tsp. quick-cooking tapioca | 2 cups peas |

1. Place raw beef cubes in a single layer in a heavy roasting pan.
2. Add vegetables, except peas. Sprinkle tapioca, salt and pepper over vegetables. Add tomato juice and water. Sprinkle brown sugar over everything.
3. Cover and bake at 325° for 2 hours.
4. Add peas and bake 1 more hour, or bake stew for 3 hours, microwave peas until cooked and stir in just before serving.

We would put this old family recipe into the oven to bake while we went to the field to work.

— *Mrs. Martha Forry, John M. Markley Meats*

# No Peek Casserole

*Makes 6 servings*

2 lbs. bite-size beef cubes
8-oz. can mushrooms (pieces and juice)
1 can cream of mushroom soup
1 pkg. dry onion soup mix
½ cup water.

1. Mix all ingredients in a greased 2-quart casserole dish and cover tightly.
2. Bake at 300° for 3 hours. Do not peek!
3. Serve over noodles or rice.

Very tasty and easy to fix. Great for covered dish carry-ins.
— *Mrs. Ada Rohrer, John M. Markley Meats*

**Variation:**
Sauté ½ lb. sliced fresh mushrooms in 2 Tbsp. butter or margarine and use in place of canned mushrooms.

# Beef-Macaroni Skillet

*Makes 6 servings*

1 lb. ground beef
1 medium onion, chopped
3 cups tomato juice
1 Tbsp. Worcestershire®
  sauce
1 Tbsp. vinegar

1 tsp. salt
⅛ tsp. pepper
1 tsp. dry mustard
1 cup elbow macaroni,
  uncooked

1. Brown beef and onion in skillet. (You may begin with frozen ground beef and thaw in skillet.)
2. Add all remaining ingredients and simmer about 20 minutes or until macaroni is done. Stir occasionally to prevent sticking.

An easy dish for unexpected company!
— *Alice Shenk, Shenk Cheese Co.*

**Variations:**
1. For low cholesterol diet, use ground turkey.
2. Add 4-oz. can mushroom pieces or ¼ lb. sliced fresh mushrooms.
3. Use different kind of pasta for variety.

# Beef Casserole

*Makes 6 servings*

**Casserole Ingredients:**
2½ lbs ground beef
1 quart Thomas's beef broth
2½ cups potatoes, diced
2 cups peas
1½ cups celery, diced
1 small onion, chopped
3 Tbsp. flour
½ cup water

**Pastry Ingredients:**
1½ cups flour
⅔ cup shortening
1 tsp. salt
4 Tbsp. milk

1. Brown ground beef in skillet. Salt and pepper to taste.
2. Cook each vegetable separately in beef broth until almost tender. Drain and save broth.
3. Mix 3 Tbsp. flour with water to make a paste. Add paste to beef broth and bring to a boil. Boil until slightly thickened, stirring constantly.
4. Combine meat, vegetables, and broth in a large baking dish.
5. To prepare pastry, cut shortening into flour. Add salt and milk and mix by hand until pastry is pliable. Roll out and layer over meat and vegetables in baking dish.
6. Cut slits in pastry for steam to escape and flute the edges.
7. Bake at 350° about ¾ hour or until crust is golden brown.

Freezes well before or after baking.

—*Ruth Mellinger, C. H. Thomas and Son*

My earliest memories of Central Market are connected to the stand operated by Ira and Bessie Neff, my uncle and aunt. This stand was in the space now occupied by Shreiner's flowers. Bessie had many loyal customers who loved her because she believed in giving an extra measure of everything she sold. For example, a quarter peck of spinach always received an extra bunch before it was wrapped for the customer.

—*Paul L. Neff, S. Clyde Weaver, Inc.*

## Savory Sausage and Potato Pie

*Makes 6 servings*

*Crust Ingredients:*
5 medium potatoes
1 tsp. salt
1 egg, beaten
½ cup onion, finely chopped
½ cup corn flakes, crushed
2 tsp. parsley flakes

*Filling Ingredients:*
1 lb. loose sausage
½ cup green peppers, chopped
2 tsp. cornstarch or flour
1 can cream of mushroom soup
2 cups cooked corn, drained
1 cup cheese, shredded

1. Cook potatoes in salt water, peel and mash. Add egg and blend. Add onion, corn flakes and parsley. Spread mixture evenly into bottom and up the sides of an oiled 10″ pie plate or casserole dish.
2. Brown sausage in skillet. Remove and drain all but 1 Tbsp. drippings. Sauté green peppers in drippings. Stir in sausage and cornstarch or flour. Add soup and corn. Blend well and heat thoroughly.
3. Turn mixture into crust and sprinkle with cheese.
4. Bake at 400° for 25 minutes.

—*Judith E. Martin, Paul L. Sensenig and Sons*

## Sausage Casserole

*Makes 6 – 8 servings*

4 eggs
2 cups milk
2 quarts soft bread cubes
4 Tbsp. butter, melted
1 Tbsp. parsley, chopped
1 tsp. onion, minced

1 tsp. salt
1 tsp. sage or poultry seasoning
1 lb. sausage meat
1½ cups frozen peas
2 small potatoes, chopped

1. Beat eggs. Add milk. Pour over bread cubes.
2. Combine butter and seasonings. Add to bread cubes and mix well.
3. Brown sausage in a skillet. Drain off excess fat. Mix bread filling with sausage, peas and potatoes.
4. Place in greased baking dish and bake at 350° for 45 minutes.

—*Doris Reinhart, D. M. Weaver and Sons, Inc.*

# Choucroute Garnie

*Makes 4 – 6 servings*

3 Tbsp. lard or vegetable oil
½ lb. thickly sliced double smoked bacon cut into 1″-squares
2 medium onions, halved and sliced crosswise
2 cloves garlic, minced
2 lbs. prepared sauerkraut, rinsed
2 medium apples, peeled, cored and grated
1 potato, peeled and grated
1 cup dry white wine
½ cup apple cider or juice
½ cup chicken broth or water
½ tsp. dried thyme, crumbled
1 bay leaf
8 bruised juniper berries or 1 Tbsp. gin
3 cloves
pinch of salt
4 – 6 (about 1½ lbs.) knockwurst (or good quality frankfurters)
4 – 6 (about ¾ to 1¼ lbs.) weisswurst

1. Heat lard in large casserole over medium heat. Add bacon and sauté until browned (about 8 minutes). Remove bacon and reserve.
2. Add onion and more lard to casserole if necessary. Lower heat. Sauté onions until soft, not browned. Add garlic and toss until fragrant. Add sauerkraut, apple and potato and toss 2 minutes. Add wine, apple cider, broth, thyme, bay leaf, juniper berries or gin, cloves and salt to taste. Cover and simmer 30 – 35 minutes.
3. Prick sausages all over with fork. Tuck sausages into sauerkraut. Add reserved bacon. Cover and simmer another 30 minutes or until sausages are heated through.
4. Correct seasonings.

Serve with an assortment of mustards, pickles, boiled potatoes, dark bread, beer or light wine. Follow with a salad. Excellent for New Year's Day or Super Bowl meal!

— *Christine Weiss, German Deli*

# Cottage Ham and String Beans

*Makes 6 – 8 servings*

2 – 3 lb. boneless pork shoulder butt
1½ lbs. yellow string beans
1½ lbs. green string beans (or use all green beans)
1 red onion, chopped
1 carrot, chopped
3 cloves garlic, peeled but left whole
¼ cup olive oil
2 lbs. fresh plum tomatoes (or use canned and drain them)
2 tsp. dried basil leaves (or use fresh basil leaves)
salt and pepper to taste

1. Snap ends of beans and soak in cold water for 1 hour.
2. In Dutch oven sauté onion, carrot and garlic in olive oil until soft. Add string beans and nestle ham in middle. Top with plum tomatoes and basil leaves. Do not add water (beans shed their own liquid).
3. Cook covered 1 hour or until ham is cooked through.

This dish utilizes ingredients which are generally available at Central Market all year long.

— *Regine Ibold, The Spice Stand*

# Snitz and Knepp

*Makes 8 servings*

**Snitz Ingredients:**
1½ lbs. cured ham or 1 ham
   hock
2 cups dried tart apples
2 Tbsp. brown sugar

**Knepp Ingredients:**
2 cups flour
3½ tsp. baking powder
½ tsp. salt
1 egg, beaten
2 Tbsp. butter, melted
⅓ — ½ cup milk

1. Cover dried apples with water and soak overnight.
2. In the morning cover ham with cold water and cook slowly for 3 hours. Add brown sugar and cook 1 hour longer.
3. Sift together all dry ingredients. Stir in beaten egg and melted butter. Add milk to make a batter stiff enough to drop from a spoon.
4. Add apples to boiling ham. Drop batter (knepp) by spoonfuls into boiling ham and apples.
5. Cover pan tightly and cook snitz and knepp 10 to 12 more minutes. Do not lift cover until ready to serve.

— *Paul B. Martin, Spring Glen Farm Kitchen, Inc*

◆

# Ham Zucchini Potato Dish

*Makes 6 servings*

**2 lbs. ham, cubed**
**1½ cups water**
**5 medium potatoes, sliced thin**
**3 medium zucchini, sliced thin**
**8 oz. cheese, grated**
**pepper to taste**

1. Brown ham in skillet in ½ cup water. After browning, add 1 more cup water to make a tasty broth.
2. Add potatoes and zucchini and cook about 15 minutes or until vegetables are soft. Sprinkle with cheese and pepper and serve.
— *Marilyn Denlinger, Irwin S. Widders Produce*

# Asparagus Ham Bake

*Makes 6 – 8 servings*

**¾ cup milk**
**1 cup cream of mushroom soup**
**2 cups ham cubes, cooked**
**3 Tbsp. onion, chopped**
**1 cup rice, cooked**
**3 cups fresh asparagus, diced**
**½ cup sharp cheese, shredded**
**1½ cups bread crumbs, buttered**

1. Combine milk, soup, ham, onion and rice.
2. Spoon half of this mixture into a greased baking dish. Top with half of asparagus. Repeat.
3. Top with cheese and bread crumbs.
4. Bake at 375° for 45 minutes or until asparagus is done.

Wonderful asparagus taste!

# Chicken Casserole

*Makes 6 servings*

2 cups cooked chicken, diced
6 cups fresh bread cubes
¼ cup onion, diced
½ cup celery, diced
½ cup mayonnaise
½ tsp. salt

½ tsp. pepper
2 eggs
1½ cups milk
1 can cream of mushroom
  soup
¼ lb. cheese, sliced

1. Mix all ingredients except mushroom soup and cheese. Put in baking dish and let stand for one hour or refrigerate overnight.
2. Top casserole with soup and cheese. Bake at 325° for 1 hour.

This tasty dish may be prepared the day before.
— *Thelma Thomas, Willow Valley Farms*

# Lattice Top Chicken Bake

*Makes 4 – 6 servings*

1 lb. fresh or frozen broccoli
1 lb. fresh or frozen cauliflower
1 lb. fresh or frozen carrots,
  sliced
1 can cream of chicken soup
¾ cup milk
¼ tsp. seasoned salt

2 cups cooked chicken,
  chopped
1 cup cheddar cheese,
  shredded
1 onion, chopped
1 cup biscuit mix
1 egg, lightly beaten
¼ cup milk

1. Parboil fresh vegetables or thaw and drain vegetables if frozen.
2. Combine soup, milk, salt, chicken, vegetables, ½ cup cheese and half of onions.
3. Spread mixture into a greased 8″ × 12″ baking dish.
4. Combine biscuit mix, egg and milk to form a soft dough.
5. Spoon over hot chicken mixture to form a lattice design. Bake uncovered at 350° for 10–15 minutes.
6. Top with remaining cheese and onions and bake 3–5 minutes more until cheese melts and onions are lightly browned.

Good for Sunday dinner!
— *Louella E. Groff, C. Z. Martin Sons*

# Chicken and Sauerkraut

*Makes 4 – 6 servings*

**1 whole chicken**
**1 – 2 qts. sauerkraut**
**salt to taste**

1. Remove skin from chicken and cut into pieces.
2. Put pieces of chicken in bottom of crockpot. Add sauerkraut
and press down until juice comes to top. Season with salt as desired.
3. Cook all day on low heat or half day on high heat.

Great timesaver on a busy day!

—*Ruth Martin, C. Z. Martin Sons*

# Chicken Stuffing Casserole

*Makes 8 servings*

**4 – 5 medium chicken breasts (skinned if you like)**
**2 cans cream of chicken soup**
**½ cup chicken broth**
**16-oz. pkg. herb stuffing mix or your own stuffing recipe**
**½ cup chicken broth (optional)**

1. Cook chicken breasts until tender.
2. Dice chicken breasts into bite-sized pieces and mix with soup
and ½ cup broth.
3. Place chicken mixture in bottom of greased casserole dish.
4. Follow directions for making herb stuffing or use your own
stuffing recipe.
5. Put stuffing mix on top of chicken (pour ½ cup broth over for a
softer stuffing) and bake uncovered at 325° for 30 – 40 minutes.

Great for family dinners or picnics.

—*Doris Herr, customer of Bitners*

**Variation:**
Sprinkle chicken with chopped parsley before adding stuffing.

# Chicken Sour Cream Casserole

*Makes 8 servings*

**4 whole chicken breasts**
**8 oz. sour cream**
**1 can cream of chicken soup**
**2 cups Ritz® cracker crumbs**
**4 Tbsp. margarine, melted**

1. Cook chicken breasts and cut in small pieces.
2. Mix chopped chicken, sour cream and soup together. Spoon into greased baking dish.
3. Pour margarine over cracker crumbs and spoon over chicken mixture in baking dish.
4. Bake at 350° for 30 minutes.

— *Thelma Kauffman, Willow Valley Farms*

**Variation:**

1. Sprinkle 1 Tbsp. poppy seeds over casserole before baking.
2. Add 1 lb. frozen vegetable medley before putting on cracker topping.

— *Rose Meck, Robert S. Meck*

# Crab Casserole

*Makes 10–12 servings*

**¼ lb. butter**
**½ lb. cheese, grated**
**1 cup milk**
**1 Tbsp. flour**

**1 lb. crab meat**
**pepper and paprika to taste**
**cracker crumbs**

1. Melt butter. Add cheese and melt, stirring constantly.
2. Stir in ¾ cup milk. Thicken mixture with flour which has been mixed with ¼ cup milk.
3. Add crab meat and seasonings to mixture.
4. Top with cracker crumbs and bake at 325° for 1 hour.

— *Sara Jane Wenger, Tom's Flower Garden*

# Tuna Spinach Casserole

*Makes 4 servings*

2 7-oz. cans tuna, drained
2 10-oz. pkgs. frozen
   spinach, chopped
2 Tbsp. lemon juice
6 Tbsp. cheese, grated
⅔ cup bread crumbs

½ tsp. salt
1 tsp. nutmeg
dash of pepper
1 cup mayonnaise
1 large tomato

1. Cook and drain spinach.
2. Combine tuna, lemon juice, 4 Tbsp. cheese, bread crumbs, salt, nutmeg and pepper. Add spinach and mix well. Fold in mayonnaise.
3. Place mixture in 1-quart, greased casserole dish and cover with thinly sliced tomato. Sprinkle remaining cheese over tomatoes.
4. Bake at 350° for 20 minutes.

*—Cynthia Strube, Marion Cheese*

# Spinach Casserole

*Makes 6 servings*

2 lb. fresh spinach (or 4
   10-oz. pkgs. frozen)
3 Tbsp. butter
½ cup onion, chopped
1 cup bread crumbs, buttered

2 Tbsp. flour
1 cup milk
1 cup cheddar cheese, grated

1. Steam spinach until wilted (or thaw and squeeze dry). Drain.
2. Heat butter and sauté onion until tender (not brown). Add flour. Blend gradually and add milk, stirring constantly. Add cheese and heat until melted.
3. Place steamed spinach in a greased casserole. Pour cheese sauce over spinach and top with bread crumbs.
4. Bake at 400° for 20–30 minutes.

*—Ethel Stoner, John R. Stoner Vegetables*

> **During the Depression, I sold two dozen eggs for 25 cents and a pound of butter for 25 cents. Everything I sold from the stand in those days was produced on the farm.**
> *—Mabel Haverstick, Viv's Varieties*

# Zucchini Stuffing Casserole

*Makes 8 servings*

8 cups unpeeled zucchini, sliced
¼ cup onion, chopped
1 can cream of chicken soup
1 cup sour cream
1 cup carrots, shredded
½ cup butter or margarine
8-oz. pkg. herb stuffing mix

1. Cook zucchini and onion in salted boiling water for 5 minutes. Drain.
2. In separate dish mix soup and sour cream. Stir carrots into mixture. Fold in zucchini and onion.
3. Melt butter or margarine and combine with stuffing. Put half of stuffing into casserole. Spread with zucchini mixture. Top with remaining stuffing.
4. Bake at 350° for 25 minutes
*—Joanne Mylin, Irwin S. Widders Produce*

**Variation:**
Add browned hamburger as an additional layer on top of the vegetables.

# Zucchini Mushroom Casserole

*Makes 6 servings*

4 cups zucchini squash, finely grated
1 medium onion, diced
1 can cream of mushroom soup
1 egg, beaten
salt and pepper to taste
1 cup bread crumbs
¼ lb. cheese, grated

1. Mix together all ingredients except cheese and bread crumbs.
2. Spoon into 2-quart greased casserole dish and top with bread crumbs and cheese.
3. Bake at 350° for 30–35 minutes.
*—Elva Martin, Rudolph Breighner*

◆

# Cauliflower Casserole

*Casserole Ingredients:*
1 large head cauliflower
2 hard-boiled eggs
½ tsp. salt
¼ tsp. pepper
¼ cup Velveeta® cheese,
  cubed
½ cup buttered bread
  crumbs

*White Sauce Ingredients:*
4 Tbsp. butter
4 Tbsp. flour
1 tsp. salt
2 cups milk

1. To prepare white sauce, melt butter in heavy sauce pan. Add flour and salt and stir until well blended. Slowly add milk, stirring constantly. Stir until a smooth paste is formed.
2. Cut head of cauliflower into flowerets and cook until soft. Drain.
3. Mix all ingredients for the casserole thoroughly. Add white sauce to mixture and mix well. Pour into greased 1½-quart casserole dish. Place bread crumbs on top.
4. Bake at 375° for 25 minutes.

— *Ruth Thomas, Helen Thomas Produce*

**Variation:**
Substitute broccoli for cauliflower.

# Broccoli Rice Dish

*Makes 6 servings*

½ cup regular rice or 1 cup minute rice
4 Tbsp. margarine
1 cup celery, chopped
1 small onion, chopped
10-oz. pkg. chopped broccoli, thawed
1 can cream of mushroom soup
1 cup sharp cheese, grated
1 cup buttered bread crumbs or crushed corn flakes

1. Cook rice according to directions.
2. Sauté onion and celery in margarine until tender.
3. Thoroughly mix all ingredients except bread crumbs or corn flakes.
4. Pour into greased casserole dish and top with bread crumbs or crushed corn flakes.
5. Bake at 350° for ½ hour.

— *Sara Jane Wenger, Tom's Flower Garden*

# Sweet Potato Pudding

*Makes 6 servings*

| | |
|---|---|
| 2 cups mashed sweet potatoes | 1 cup milk |
| 6 Tbsp. brown sugar | 2 eggs |
| 1 tsp. salt | 1 cup miniature marshmallows |
| 2 tsp. butter, melted | |

1. Cook sweet potatoes in skins until soft. Peel and mash. Add sugar, salt, melted butter and milk. (It is best to add ingredients while potatoes are still hot.) Add eggs and beat well with mixer.
2. Pour into a greased baking dish. Top casserole with marshmallows and bake at 350° for 45 minutes or until center is completely set.

This dish may be prepared in advance. Great for Thanksgiving and Christmas dinner.

— *Ruth Widders, Irwin S. Widders Produce*

# Sweet Potato Casserole

*Makes 6 servings*

| *Sweet Potato Ingredients:* | *Topping Ingredients:* |
|---|---|
| 3 cups cooked and mashed sweet potatoes | 1 cup brown sugar |
| ⅓ cup sugar | ⅓ cup flour |
| 2 eggs | ⅓ cup margarine, softened |
| 1 tsp. vanilla | 1 cup pecans, chopped |
| ½ cup milk | |
| ½ cup margarine, melted | |

1. After mashing sweet potatoes add sugar, eggs, vanilla, milk and melted margarine. Mix well.
2. Cut brown sugar, flour and margarine together until crumbly. Add chopped pecans.
3. Place sweet potato mixture in a greased casserole. Top with pecan mixture.
4. Bake at 350° for 30 minutes.

— *Patricia A. Carter, McComsey Family*

◆

# Sweet Potato and Apple Casserole

*Makes 6 servings*

6 sweet potatoes
2 cups apple slices, peeled
½ cup brown sugar, firmly packed
½ tsp. salt
2 Tbsp. butter

1. Cook sweet potatoes until tender. Peel and cut into slices.
2. Grease a 2-quart casserole dish and in it arrange alternating layers of sweet potatoes and apple slices. Sprinkle brown sugar and salt over casserole. Dot with 2 Tbsp. butter.
3. Bake uncovered at 350° for 50 minutes.

Great potato dish for Thanksgiving!

—*Rose Meck, Robert S. Meck*

# Easy Eggplant Casserole

*Makes 8 servings*

1 medium eggplant
salt and pepper to taste
1 medium onion, chopped
1 cup fresh mushrooms,
  sliced
1 – 2 Tbsp. butter

1 – 2 cans cream of mush-
  room soup
1 cup buttered bread crumbs
¼ tsp. garlic salt
¼ tsp. paprika
1½ cups cheese, grated

1. Pare, dice and cook eggplant until soft. Salt and pepper to taste. Drain. Place in greased 7″ × 11″ baking dish.
2. Sauté onion and mushrooms in butter. Add mushroom soup and pour over eggplant. Season bread crumbs with garlic salt and paprika. Cover casserole with layer of cheese and buttered bread crumbs.
3. Bake at 350° for 30 minutes.

—*Ethel Stoner, John R. Stoner Vegetables*

# Baked Eggplant Casserole

*Makes 6 – 8 servings*

2 cups eggplant, cubed
2 eggs, beaten
2 Tbsp. flour
2 Tbsp. butter
1 cup milk
1 small onion, finely
   chopped

2 slices bread torn into cubes
1 tsp. salt
1 Tbsp. ketchup
¼ tsp. pepper
1 cup sharp cheese, shredded

1. Mix thoroughly all ingredients except cheese.
2. Pour into greased casserole. Top with cheese.
3. Bake at 350° for 30 minutes.

—*Mildred Brackbill, Utz's Potato Chips*

# A Greek Delicacy

*Makes 8 entree servings*
*Makes 12 – 20 appetizer servings*

3 Tbsp. butter
½ cup flour
4 cups milk
1¼ lbs. feta cheese,
   crumbled

1 cup asiago cheese, grated
6 eggs, lightly beaten
1 lb. phyllo dough
1 cup butter or margarine,
   melted

1. Melt 3 Tbsp. butter. Add flour and blend, browning slightly.
Add milk and cook mixture until thick. Cool.
2. To cooled mixture add crumbled feta, grated asiago and beaten
eggs.
3. Line a 9″ × 13″ baking dish with 3 layers of phyllo dough and
paint with butter. Add 3 more layers of dough and paint with butter.
4. Pour liquid cheese mixture over phyllo dough. Top with 3 more
layers of dough and paint with butter. Continue to alternate 3
layers of phyllo dough, painting with butter each time, until entire
pound of dough has been used.
5. Bake 45 minutes at 300°.

This recipe was given to us by a Greek friend whose family was
from Northern Greece.

—*Sam Neff, S. Clyde Weaver, Inc.*

◆

# Aunt Vera Weaver's
# Baked Cheese Soufflé

*Makes 4 servings*

1 cup dry bread cubes (¾–1″ square)
1 cup medium sharp Colby cheese, diced
1 Tbsp. butter, melted
3 eggs, separated
½ tsp. salt
1 cup milk

1. Mix bread with cheese and butter. Add well-beaten egg yolks and salt. Mix together.
2. Heat milk to scalding. Pour over bread mixture and stir until mixed.
3. Beat eggs whites until very stiff. Fold into bread and cheese mixture.
4. Pour soufflé into a small greased casserole and bake at 350° for 35 minutes.

I remember how this came out of Mother's oven "high," and by the time the family gathered around the table, the fondue, as we called it, had settled.

— *Sam Neff, S. Clyde Weaver Inc.*

# Springtime Quiche

*Makes 12–16 servings*

2 9-inch pie shells
1 egg white, slightly beaten
1½ lbs. fresh asparagus
1 tsp. salt
8 slices bacon

½ lb. Swiss cheese, grated
4 eggs
1½ cups half and half
dash nutmeg
salt and pepper to taste
10 cherry tomatoes, halved

1. Brush pie shell with egg white.
2. Wash asparagus, cut off tough ends and set aside the 16 best spears (5 inches long). Cut remaining spears into pieces and cook in salt water 5 minutes. Drain and rinse in cold water.
3. Fry, drain and crumble bacon. Sprinkle bottom of pie shell with bacon, cheese, and cooked asparagus pieces.
4. Mix beaten eggs, half and half, nutmeg, salt and pepper together. Pour mixture into pie shell.
5. Arrange asparagus spears and cherry tomato halves spoke-fashion on pie shell.
6. Bake at 400° for 35 minutes or until firm.

— *Ethel Stoner, John R. Stoner Vegetables*

# Quiche Lorraine

*Makes 6 servings*

| | |
|---|---|
| ½ lb. bacon | 2 cups cream |
| 1 cup Swiss cheese, grated | ¾ tsp. salt |
| 1 Tbsp. onion, grated | ¼ tsp. sugar |
| 4 eggs, beaten | 1 9″ unbaked pie shell |

1. Use favorite pie crust recipe for pastry. Place in a 9-inch pie pan.
2. Fry and crumble bacon. Sprinkle bacon, onion and cheese into pastry-lined pie plate.
3. Combine eggs, cream, salt and sugar and mix well. Pour mixture into pie plate.
4. Bake 15 minutes at 425°. Reduce temperature to 300° and bake 30 minutes longer or until knife inserted in center comes out clean.

*—Joyce Deiter, Eisenberger's Baked Goods*

# Asparagus Mushroom Casserole

*Makes 6 servings*

| | |
|---|---|
| 2 lbs. fresh asparagus | 3 cups milk |
| ½ lb. mushrooms, cleaned and sliced | 1 tsp. salt |
| | 1 tsp. chives |
| 2 Tbsp. margarine | 2 tsp. pimento, finely chopped |
| 6 Tbsp. margarine, melted | |
| 6 Tbsp. flour | 3 hard-boiled eggs, sliced |
| | 1 cup buttered bread crumbs |

1. Cut asparagus in pieces and cook until tender. Set aside.
2. Sauté mushrooms in 2 Tbsp. margarine. Set aside.
3. Melt 6 Tbsp. margarine in heavy saucepan. Blend in flour, cooking and stirring until mixture is bubbly. Slowly add milk, stirring constantly. Heat until white sauce is thickened and smooth. Remove from heat and add salt, chives and pimento.
4. Stir mushrooms and eggs into white sauce.
5. Place drained asparagus in greased 2-quart casserole dish. Cover with mushroom and white sauce mixture.
6. Sprinkle bread crumbs over top and bake at 325° for 20 minutes.

*—Helen E. Bitner, Bitners*

# Market Rules
## 1889

1. Persons renting stalls must pay for the same before occupying them.

2. Not more than two families or the representatives of more than two separate interests will be permitted to occupy one and the same stall at one and the same time.

3. Persons renting stalls shall keep the same clean.

4. Sixty-six stalls, numbered from 1 to 66 inclusive, are set apart for the retailing of meats, and it shall be unlawful for anyone to retail fresh meats any where else within the Market limits; provided, however, that farmers who do not make a business of butchering shall have the privilege to dispose of the surplus meats, etc., after their annual butchering, at their own stall.

5. Sixteen stalls, numbered 139 to 142 inclusive, 175 to 182 inclusive, and 215 to 218 inclusive, are set apart for Bakers, for the sale of Bread, Cakes, etc., and it shall be unlawful to engage in said business anywhere else in the Market House.

6. Eight stalls, numbered 67 to 70 inclusive, and 95 to 98 inclusive, are set apart for Dried Meat and Cheese Dealers, and it shall be unlawful to carry on said business anywhere else in the Market House; provided, that farmers, who do not make a business of butchering and drying meats, shall have the privilege to dispose of their surplus dried meats after their annual butchering at their own stall, and also of selling their homemade cheese.

7. Stalls outside, on the northern side of the Market House, are set apart for the sale of Fresh Fish, during market hours only; and it shall be unlawful to sell fresh fish anywhere else in the market limits.

8. The West King Street curb and the southwest angle of Centre Square are set apart for the sale of meat in not less quantities than by the quarter.

9. Hawking or Peddling within the Market House is strictly prohibited.

10. Dogs must be kept out of the Market House, and the owners of them will be held responsible for any violation of this rule.

11. It shall be unlawful to move or push out of place any stall or stand. The number of the stall shall not be obscured, nor shall any sign be put up above or higher than said number. No additions shall be made to the stalls or stands, neither by adding nor taking away shelves or other devices. No foot boards shall be used back of the stalls; but carpets or rugs may be used to stand on; provided that they are removed at the close of the market.

12. No person shall keep any horse, cart, carriage, wagon, wheelbarrow or other vehicle in the avenues around the Market House any longer than may be necessary to unload the same and place their goods on the stalls; and all person occupying stands out of the Market House, and selling from wagons and other vehicles, shall back their vehicles against the curb stone and remove their horses as soon as possible.

13. A penalty of $10 is imposed by law for the violation of any of these rules.

Adopted by Market Committee, November 5, 1889.
Approved by Select and Common Council, November 6, 1889.

# Vegetable Lasagna

*Makes 4 – 6 servings*

6 lasagna noodles
2 Tbsp. vegetable oil
1½ cups onion, chopped
1 clove garlic, minced
1 green pepper, sliced
15-oz. can tomato sauce
15-oz. can tomato paste
1 large tomato, chopped
½ tsp. basil
1 tsp. oregano
1 lb. cottage cheese, small
  curd

1 cup Parmesan cheese,
  grated
1 egg, slightly beaten
2 10-oz. pkgs. chopped
  spinach, thawed
2 – 3 Tbsp. margarine
2½ cups zucchini, thinly
  sliced
2½ cups fresh mushrooms,
  sliced
6 oz. mozzarella cheese,
  sliced

1. Cook lasagna until tender (about 5 minutes). Drain and rinse in cold water.
2. Place oil, onion, garlic and green pepper in microwave uncovered for 2½ minutes. Add tomato sauce, tomato paste, tomatoes, basil and oregano. Mix well. Cook in microwave for 15 minutes (power 5).
3. Make a cottage cheese mixture by mixing cottage cheese, ¼ cup Parmesan cheese and beaten egg.
4. Make a spinach cheese mixture by pressing moisture out of spinach and folding in the remaining Parmesan cheese.
5. Sauté zucchini in 2 – 3 Tbsp. margarine until tender.

*To assemble lasagna:*
1. Spread layer of tomato sauce in bottom of an oiled glass dish.
2. Cover with three noodles.
3. Add ½ of zucchini, ½ of mushrooms, ½ of spinach cheese, and ½ of cottage cheese.
4. Repeat all of above steps, beginning and ending with the sauce.
5. Microwave on high (power 10) for 10 minutes covered. Reduce to medium (power 5) and cook for 17 more minutes. Uncover and cook on medium (power 5) 18 more minutes.
6. Top with mozzarella cheese, cover and let stand for 5 minutes before serving.

*—Ethel Stoner, John R. Stoner Vegetables*

**Variations:**
  1. Sauté onion, garlic and green pepper on top of stove for 5 minutes or until tender. Add tomato sauce, tomato paste, tomato, basil and oregano and mix well. Simmer for 20 minutes, covered.
  2. After lasagna is assembled, bake in conventional oven for 45 minutes at 350°. Top with mozzarella cheese and return to oven for 5 more minutes.

# Pineapple Bread Casserole

*Makes 6 – 8 servings*

¼ lb. butter (1 stick), softened
1 cup granulated sugar
4 eggs
16-oz. can crushed pineapple, drained
6 slices stale bread, cubed
pinch of salt

1. Beat butter and sugar until creamy. Add eggs and beat. Add pineapples and mix thoroughly.
2. Fold in bread cubes and salt. Spoon into well-greased baking dish.
3. Bake at 375° for 45 minutes.

Delicious with ham!

— *Anna F. Kreider, Viv's Varieties*

# Bread Filling

*Makes 4 servings*

| | |
|---|---|
| 8 Tbsp. margarine | 1 tsp. parsley flakes |
| ¼ cup onion, chopped | salt and pepper to taste |
| ¼ cup celery, chopped | pinch saffron |
| 2 eggs | 2 cups milk |
| ½ tsp. poultry seasoning | 12-oz. pkg. bread cubes |

1. Melt margarine in pan on stove. Add celery and onion and cook until tender.
2. In blender mix eggs, seasonings and milk.
3. Pour egg mixture over bread cubes and fold into margarine mixture on stove. Cook over low heat about 20 minutes, stirring occasionally.
4. Put in greased casserole dish and bake at 250° for 1 hour.

— *Mrs. Robert Funk, Funk Brothers, Inc.*

# Filled Noodles

*Makes 4 servings:*

*Dough Ingredients:*
2 cups flour
½ tsp. salt
2 eggs, lightly beaten
¼ cup cold water

*Additional Ingredients:*
3 – 4 qts. water
4 beef bouillon cubes

*Filling Ingredients:*
1 lb. ground beef
1 medium onion, finely
    chopped
¾ cup bread crumbs
1 egg, lightly beaten
salt and pepper to taste
parsley
1 Tbsp. butter

1. Thoroughly mix all filling ingredients. Divide into 4 – 6 patties.
2. To make noodle dough mix flour, salt, eggs and water. Knead with fingers until well mixed. Divide dough into 4 – 6 equal pieces.
3. On floured surface roll out dough until each piece is large and flat enough to hold and cover a meat patty. Place meat patty in center of each dough piece. Bring opposite ends of dough together and press firmly. Moisten finger with water and rub over dough to seal.
4. Bring 3 – 4 quarts water to a boil. Add bouillon cubes and parsley. Drop filled noodles into boiling water and cook for 30 minutes at a low boil.
5. Brown butter by heating slowly.
6. Remove noodles from pot to dinner plate and pour browned butter over noodles.

I grew up with this special treat.

— *Cynthia Strube, Marion Cheese*

# Dutch Noodles Florentine

*Makes 6 servings*

1 lb. bacon
1 lb. noodles
10-oz. pkg. frozen spinach
 or 1 lb. fresh spinach
½ cup butter

1 egg, lightly beaten
1½ cups heavy cream
2 cups Parmesan cheese,
 freshly grated
salt and pepper to taste

1. Cook bacon and drain it. Crumble and set aside.
2. Cook noodles according to directions.
3. If using frozen spinach, thaw and drain. If using fresh spinach, wash well and drain.
4. Melt butter in large heavy saucepan. Add spinach and heat through. Add drained noodles and toss lightly.
5. In another pan combine egg, cream, cheese, salt and pepper and heat over very low heat 5 minutes. Pour over noodle mixture and gently toss.
6. Serve in a heated dish.
 —*Mary Ellen Campbell, Baskets of Central Market*

# My Homemade Noodles

4 medium eggs
3 cups all-purpose flour

1. Beat eggs well. Add flour and mix.
2. Roll out dough as thinly as possible and cut into strips.
3. When dough has partially dried, stack the strips and cut crosswise into thin noodles. Allow to dry thoroughly, before storing.
4. Prepare noodles for serving by adding to boiling water.
 —*Mrs. William Mellinger, Shutt's Candies*

# Homemade Pizza

*Makes 6 – 8 servings*

*Crust Ingredients:*
1 Tbsp. yeast or 1 pkg. dry
   active yeast
1 cup hot water
1 tsp. salt
1 tsp. sugar
2½ cups flour
2 Tbsp. vegetable oil

*Topping Ingredients:*
1 small jar tomato sauce
1 lb. hamburger, browned
½ lb. pepperoni slices
2 green peppers, sliced
1 large onion, sliced
1 cup olives, sliced
1 lb. mozzerella cheese,
   shredded

1. Dissolve yeast in hot water. Using a fork, stir in salt and sugar.
2. Add flour ½ cup at a time, stirring with fork.
3. Add oil and stir vigorously with fork. If dough is sticky, add another ½ cup flour. Allow dough to rise for ½ hour.
4. Using floured hands knead dough, then spread out on greased cookie sheet with floured fingertips.
5. Spread tomato sauce over dough. Add hamburger, pepperoni, peppers, onions and olives in layers. Sprinkle cheese over top.
6. Bake at 425° for 20 – 25 minutes.

Young children enjoy helping to prepare this nutritious food. Our family enjoys making different-shaped pizzas. For example, hearts, small fish or other animal shapes.

— *Peggy Moyer, Donegal Gardens*

**Variations:**
1. Make your own pan pizza by following directions as given in this recipe. Bake 10 minutes in a well-greased iron skillet instead of on cookie sheet.
2. Use a variety of other toppings.

◆

# Italian Steak Sandwiches

*Makes 8 servings*

| | |
|---|---|
| 2 cups tomato juice | 2 lbs. chipped steak or |
| 6-oz. can tomato paste | hamburger |
| 2 Tbsp. spaghetti sauce | ½ cup onion, chopped |
| ⅓ cup sugar or less, as | salt and pepper to taste |
| desired | 16 slices cheese |

1. Mix together tomato juice, tomato paste, spaghetti sauce and sugar. Simmer over low heat for 1 hour.
2. Fry chipped steak or hamburger. When browned add onion, salt and pepper. Cook until onions are tender. Add the sauce and mix well, simmering for 20 minutes.
3. Put mixture into steak rolls and top each roll with several slices of cheese. Place sandwiches in oven and heat until cheese melts. Serve immediately.

Hint: Leftover sauce may be frozen for later use.

*—Joyce Deiter, Eisenberger's Baked Goods*

**Variation:**

Serve the meat and cheese in pocket bread for easier handling, especially for young children.

When I first started on market, market did not open until noon and it went until 8 o'clock at night. I think market went back to the extremely early hours during the War (1940s) when many women went back to work because their husbands were gone. We started opening earlier and earlier so they could shop before they left for work.

*—Mabel Haverstick, Viv's Varieties*

# Sausage Egg Brunch

*Makes 4 – 6 servings*

**2 cups unseasoned croutons**
**1 lb. sausage meat, cooked and drained**
**1 cup sharp cheese, grated**
**6 eggs**
**2 cups milk**
**1 Tbsp. dry mustard**

1. Layer croutons, sausage and cheese in a greased 9″ × 13″ dish.
2. Beat eggs well. Add milk and mustard and mix well. Pour over sausage. Cover and refrigerate overnight.
3. Bake at 375° for 45 minutes. Let stand 10 minutes before serving.
— *Louella E. Groff, C. Z. Martin Sons*

**Variations:**
Bacon, chipped ham or chipped dried beef may be used instead of sausage. When using bacon, fry and drain.

# Egg, Potato and Cheese Casserole

*Makes 4 – 6 servings*

**6 – 8 medium potatoes**
**8 eggs**
**2 Tbsp. water**
**3 cups sharp cheese, grated**
**salt and pepper to taste**

1. Cook potatoes and cool in the refrigerator for several hours. Peel, then grate.
2. Mix eggs, water, salt and pepper together.
3. Put potatoes evenly over bottom of a greased casserole. Pour beaten egg mixture over potatoes. Spread cheese over top.
4. Bake at 350° for 45 minutes (cover with foil for the first 30 minutes). Let set 10 minutes after baking before serving.

Delicious breakfast or brunch!
— *Joyce Deiter, Eisenberger's Baked Goods*
**Variations:**
1. Add finely diced onion to egg mixture.
2. Add browned, diced ham, sausage or bacon to egg mixture.

# Egg and Vegetable Casserole

*Makes 6 – 8 servings*

| | |
|---|---|
| 1 cup potatoes, diced | 1 tsp. salt |
| 1 cup celery, diced | 1/8 tsp. pepper |
| 1 cup carrots, diced | 2 cups milk |
| 1 small onion, minced | 4 hard-boiled eggs, sliced |
| 4 Tbsp. butter or margarine | 1/2 cup cheese, grated |
| 4 Tbsp. flour | 1/4 cup buttered bread crumbs |

1. Cook and drain potatoes, celery and carrots.
2. Sauté onion in butter or margarine until tender (not brown). Blend in flour, seasonings and milk, stirring constantly. Add drained vegetables and mix thoroughly.
3. Pour half of creamed vegetables into greased casserole and add half of sliced eggs. Repeat layers.
4. Sprinkle top with cheese and bread crumbs.
5. Bake at 400° for 15 – 20 minutes or until slightly browned.

My mother made this dish over 50 years ago and served it as a one-dish meal along with home-canned fruit. I still enjoy it.

— *Alice Shenk, Shenk Cheese Co.*

**Variation:**

Do not drain vegetables and use proportionately less milk.

# Baked Oatmeal

*Makes 4 – 5 servings*

¼ cup cooking oil
½ cup sugar
1 egg
1½ cups quick oats

1 tsp. baking powder
½ tsp. salt
½ cup milk

1. Cream oil, sugar and egg together.
2. Add all other ingredients and mix. Pour into a greased 8″-square cake pan.
3. Bake at 350° for 30 minutes. Serve with milk.

**Variations:**
    1. Add ¼ cup raisins, ¼ cup nuts and ½ tsp. cinnamon.
    2. Line bottom of cake pan with sliced apples.

For our family the variations are a must. Even those who do not enjoy oatmeal almost always love it this way.

— *Joanne Warfel, S. Clyde Weaver, Inc.*

# French Toast

*Makes 4 generous servings*

1½ cups flour
2⅔ tsp. baking powder
½ tsp. salt

1¼ cups milk
2 eggs
1 loaf challa bread

1. Sift together all dry ingredients.
2. Beat together eggs and milk. Add dry ingredients and mix well. If batter seems too thick thin with more milk.
3. Dip slices of bread into mixture. Deep fry in cooking oil which has been heated to 375°.

Hint: Coat leftover bread with powdered sugar and eat like doughnuts.

— *Hilda M. Funk, Givant's Bakery*

PIES

# Strawberry Snowbank Pie

*Makes 1 9" pie*

| | |
|---|---|
| 1 quart strawberries | 2 egg whites |
| 1¼ cups sugar | pinch of salt |
| ½ cup water | ¼ tsp. almond extract |
| ½ tsp. cream of tartar | 1 9" baked pie shell |

1. Wash, hull and drain berries. Fill pie shell with whole, unsweetened berries. Put the prettiest berries in center.
2. Mix sugar, water and cream of tartar in saucepan. Cover and bring to a boil. Uncover and cook until syrup spins long threads (240° on candy thermometer).
3. Stiffly beat egg whites and salt them. Gradually pour sugar mixture into egg whites, beating constantly. Beat until mixture piles into peaks. Add almond extract.
4. Pile icing onto pie, leaving center uncovered. Cool. Do not put into refrigerator.

*—Esther Groff, Kiefer's Meats and Cheese*

# Fresh Strawberry Pie

*Makes 1 9" pie*

| | |
|---|---|
| 1 quart fresh strawberries | ¼ tsp. salt |
| 1 cup sugar | 1 Tbsp. lemon juice |
| 1¼ cups water | 3-oz. pkg. strawberry gelatin |
| 4 Tbsp. cornstarch | 1 9" baked pie shell |

1. Dissolve sugar in ½ cup water and bring to a boil. In separate container mix remaining ¾ cup water with cornstarch. Stir to form a smooth paste.
2. Add cornstarch to boiling sugar water and stir. Add all other ingredients except strawberries. Heat, stirring constantly, until mixture is thick and transparent.
3. Place strawberries in pie shell.
4. Pour glaze over berries. Garnish.

Valentine's Day is a special time to serve fresh strawberry pie. Our stand has fresh Florida and California strawberries in February.

*—Rose Meck, Robert S. Meck*

◆

# Fresh Banana Rhubarb Pie

*Makes 1 9" pie*

½ lb. fresh rhubarb
3 medium ripe bananas
1 cup sugar
¼ cup orange juice, freshly
squeezed
3 Tbsp. flour

¼ tsp. salt
¼ tsp. cinnamon
1 tsp. nutmeg
1 Tbsp. butter or margarine
1 9" unbaked double pie
crust

1. Prepare pastry. Roll out half of pastry to fit pie plate.
2. Slice rhubarb (should yield about 3 cups). Slice bananas (should yield about 3 cups).
3. Combine rhubarb, bananas, sugar, orange juice, flour, salt and spices. Spread into pie plate. Dot with butter.
4. Place crust on top.
5. Bake at 450° for 15 minutes. Reduce oven temperature to 350° and bake 20 minutes longer until golden brown.

*—Mabel Haverstick, Viv's Varieties*

# Rhubarb Meringue Pie

Makes 1 9" pie

**Pie Ingredients:**
3 cups fresh rhubarb
1 cup sugar
2 Tbsp. flour
1 Tbsp. water
⅛ tsp. salt
3 egg yolks, well beaten
1 9" unbaked pie shell

**Meringue Ingredients:**
3 egg whites
4 Tbsp. sugar

1. Fill pie shell with fresh rhubarb cut into slices.
2. Thoroughly mix all other pie ingredients and pour over rhubarb. Bake at 400° for 30 minutes. Reduce oven temperature to 350° and bake for 30 more minutes.
3. To prepare meringue beat egg whites until stiff. Add sugar and beat until well mixed. Spread over pie and return pie to oven for 15 minutes at 350° or until meringue is brown.

*—Margaret Groff, friend of Helen E. Bitner*

# Mother Stover's Peach Pie

*Makes 2 9″ pies*

| | |
|---|---|
| 8 peaches | 2 Tbsp. butter, melted |
| 3 eggs | cinnamon |
| ¾ cup sugar | 2 9″ unbaked pie shells |
| 4 Tbsp. flour | |

1. Peel and dice peaches. Separate the eggs.
2. Brush pie shells with some of the egg white. Bake shells (weighted with rice or dried beans) at 350° until lightly brown.
3. Blend sugar, flour and butter. Add egg yolks. Beat egg whites until stiff. Fold into mixture.
4. Put diced peaches into partially baked pie shells. Pour mixture over peaches and sprinkle with cinnamon.
5. Bake at 425° for 15 minutes. Reduce oven temperature to 325° and bake for another 30 minutes.

This is my mother-in-law's recipe from Franklin County. When peaches are in season, this pie is fabulous.
— *Sam Neff, S. Clyde Weaver, Inc.*

# Orange Pie

*Makes 2 9″ pies*

| | |
|---|---|
| 8 Tbsp. butter | 2 cups milk |
| 1 orange, cut fine | ¼ cup flour |
| 1 cup sugar | 2 egg whites |
| 2 egg yolks | 2 9″ unbaked pie shells |

1. Melt butter and brown slightly.
2. Thoroughly mix all ingredients except egg whites.
3. Beat egg whites until stiff and fold into pie filling.
4. Pour into pie shells and bake at 350° for 30–35 minutes.
— *Doris Reinhart, D. M. Weaver and Sons, Inc.*

> **Wherever we travel we always visit the public market-places. We have found these are great places to touch the local culture. You see how people live and what they eat.**
> — *Paul L., Anna Mary and Sam Neff, S. Clyde Weaver, Inc.*

◆

# Concord Grape Pie

*Makes 1 9" pie*

*Pie Filling Ingredients:*

4 cups grapes
1 cup sugar
⅓ cup flour
¼ tsp. salt

2 Tbsp. butter, melted
1 Tbsp. lemon juice
1 9" unbaked pie shell

*Crumb Topping Ingredients:*

½ cup flour
½ cup sugar
¼ cup butter or margarine, softened

1. Slip skins from grapes. Set skins aside. Bring pulp of grapes to a boil. Reduce heat and simmer for 5 minutes.
2. Remove from heat and put through food press to separate seeds from pulp. Stir pulp and skins together.
3. Combine sugar, flour and salt. Add melted butter and lemon juice to dry ingredients. Add grapes and mix well.
4. Spoon into unbaked pie shell.
5. To prepare crumb topping sift flour with sugar. Cut butter or margarine into mixture until it is crumbly. Sprinkle topping over pie filling.
6. Bake at 400° for 40 minutes.

Unusual and delicious!

— *Doris Shenk, Donegal Gardens*
— *Ruth Widders, Irwin S. Widders Produce*

# Blueberry Pie

*Makes 1 9" pie*

6 cups blueberries
½ cup water
1 cup sugar

1 Tbsp. butter or margarine
4 Tbsp. cornstarch
1 9" unbaked pie shell

1. Combine blueberries, water, sugar and butter or margarine in saucepan and bring to a boil. Add cornstarch and boil until mixture is clear.
2. Cool mixture and place into unbaked pie shell.
3. Bake at 425° for 10 minutes. Reduce oven temperature to 375° and bake another 20 minutes. Cool and serve.

A family favorite when served with vanilla ice cream!
— *Joyce Deiter, Eisenberger's Baked Goods*

# Lemon Sponge Pie

*Makes 1 8" pie*

2 Tbsp. butter, softened
1 cup sugar
3 Tbsp. flour
½ tsp. salt

3 eggs, separated
juice and rind of one lemon
1½ cups milk
1 8" unbaked pie shell

1. Cream butter and sugar together. Add flour and salt.
2. Separate the eggs and add egg yolks to mixture. Add lemon juice, grated rind and milk.
3. Beat egg whites and fold into mixture.
4. Pour into an unbaked pie shell and bake at 325° for 40 to 45 minutes.

*— Ruth Eshleman, Givant's Bakery*

# Dried Snitz Pie

*Makes 1 9" pie*

2 cups dried tart apples
1½ cups warm water
⅔ cup sugar
½ tsp. powdered cloves

½ tsp. cinnamon
1 9" unbaked double pie
crust

1. Soak apples in warm water. Cook over low heat until soft.
2. When apples are soft, drain in a colander, pressing them to remove water.
3. Add sugar and spices to apples. Put mixture in an unbaked pie shell. Cover pie with a top crust; fasten at edges.
4. Bake at 425° for 15 minutes. Reduce oven temperature to 375° and continue to bake for 35 minutes.

*— Charles Hess*

◆

# Greatest Apple Pie

*Makes 1 9" pie*

¾–1 cup sugar
2 Tbsp. flour
½–1 tsp. cinnamon
dash nutmeg and salt

6 cups apples, sliced
2 Tbsp. butter
1 9" unbaked double pie
  crust

1. Combine sugar, flour, cinnamon, nutmeg and salt. Add sliced apples and mix well.
2. Fill pie plate with apple mixture and dot with butter.
3. Cover with a top crust.
4. Bake at 400° for 55 minutes. Serve warm.

Makes an easy lunch with a sandwich.

— *Doris Shenk, Donegal Gardens*

**Variation:**
   Cover with crumb topping instead of top crust.

# Cherry Cream Pie

*Makes 1 9" pie*

15-oz. can condensed sweetened milk
⅓ cup lemon juice
1 tsp. vanilla
½ tsp. almond extract
½ cup whipping cream, whipped
1 can cherry pie filling
1 9" unbaked pie shell

1. Bake pie shell (weighted with rice or dried beans) at 375° for 30 minutes. Let it cool.
2. Combine condensed milk, lemon juice, vanilla and almond extract. Stir well until mixture thickens.
3. Fold whipped cream into mixture and spoon into cooled pie shell. Top mixture with pie filling.
4. Chill 2–3 hours and serve.

— *Mrs. Robert Funk, Funk Brothers, Inc.*

**Variation:**
   Use blueberry pie filling.

# Pumpkin Delight Pie

*Makes 1 9" pie*

1 pint Shenk's Pumpkin Delight
2 Tbsp. flour
½ tsp. salt
2 eggs, slightly beaten
1 cup evaporated milk
½ tsp. vanilla extract
½ – 1 tsp. cinnamon (optional)
1 9" unbaked pie shell

1. Combine Pumpkin Delight, flour and salt. Add eggs and mix well. Stir in evaporated milk and vanilla. Also add cinnamon, if desired.
2. Pour into pie shell and bake at 375° for 45 – 50 minutes.
3. Serve cold with whipped topping.

Shenk's Pumpkin Delight is a new product and this is a "different tasting" pie. It may be purchased from Shenk's Cheese Co. at Central Market.

— *Alice Shenk, Shenk's Cheese Co.*

**Variation:**
If unable to get Pumpkin Delight, use 1 pint pumpkin, ½ cup brown sugar and ¼ cup granulated sugar.

# Pumpkin Pie

*Makes 2 9" pies*

1 cup cooked pumpkin
1 cup sugar
4 eggs, separated
½ cup flour
2 tsp. pumpkin pie spice
2 Tbsp. butter, melted
4 cups warm milk
2 9" unbaked pie shells

1. Mix pumpkin, sugar and egg yolks. Stir in flour and spice. Add melted butter and warm milk. Mix well.
2. Beat egg whites until stiff. Fold into pumpkin mix. Pour into two unbaked pie shells.
3. Bake at 450° for 10 minutes. Reduce oven temperature to 325° and bake for 30 more minutes.
4. Serve with whipped topping, if desired.

— *Ann Kreider, Viv's Varieties*

◆

# Raisin Cream Pie

*Makes 1 8" pie*

**Filling Ingredients:**
¾ cup brown sugar
5 Tbsp. cornstarch
2¼ cups milk
2 egg yolks
1 Tbsp. butter
1 Tbsp. vanilla
1 cup raisins
1 8" baked pie shell

**Meringue Ingredients:**
3 egg whites
½ tsp. vanilla
¼ tsp. cream of tartar
6 Tbsp. sugar

1. Mix brown sugar, cornstarch and ¼ cup milk until smooth. Then add remaining milk and bring mixture to a boil in a double boiler. Add egg yolks, butter, vanilla and raisins.
2. Remove from heat and pour mixture into a baked pie shell.
3. Prepare meringue by beating egg whites with vanilla and cream of tartar. Gradually add sugar and beat until mixture forms peaks.
4. Spread meringue over pie and put under broiler until meringue is brown. (Watch carefully to prevent burning!)

*—Doris Shenk, Donegal Gardens*

# Raisin Pie

*Makes 1 8" pie*

1 cup sugar
1 cup raisins
1 Tbsp. flour
1 Tbsp. vinegar

1 Tbsp. butter
dash of salt
1½ cups boiling water
2 8" unbaked pie shells

1. Mix all ingredients except water. Pour boiling water over mixture and stir well. Let mixture set while preparing pie shells.
2. Mixture will seem thin. Do not add anything to thicken as mixture will set as it bakes.
3. Bake at 375° for ½ hour.

*—Patricia A. Carter, McComsey Family*

# Butterscotch Pie

*Makes 1 9" pie*

*Pie Ingredients:*
2 Tbsp. butter
2 cups milk
2 egg yolks
⅓ cup flour

⅛ tsp. salt
1 cup brown sugar, firmly
    packed
½ tsp. vanilla
1 9" baked pie shell

*Topping Ingredients:*
2 egg whites
2 Tbsp. sugar
pinch of cream of tartar

1. Melt butter in a saucepan. Add all other pie ingredients and bring to a boil, stirring constantly. Continue stirring until mixture thickens. Pour into baked pie shell. Cool.
2. Beat egg whites to peaks. Add sugar and cream of tartar. Spread meringue over pie and put into oven to brown.

I enjoy this recipe because I received it from a dear friend and it is delicious.

— *Ella Porter, Hidden Acres Flowers*

# Peanut Butter Pie

*Makes 1 9" pie*

4 ozs. cream cheese
½ – 1 cup peanut butter, according to taste preference
½ cup milk
1 cup confectioner's sugar
8 ozs. whipped topping
9" graham cracker crust

1. Soften cream cheese to room temperature. Beat cream cheese, peanut butter, milk and sugar together with electric mixer. Mix until well blended. Fold whipped topping into mixture and pour into graham cracker crust.
2. Freeze for at least four hours. Remove from freezer and let stand about 10 minutes before serving.
3. Serve with shaved chocolate or chocolate syrup, if desired.

— *Mary Lou Graby, Spring Glen Farm Kitchens, Inc.*

# Shoo-Fly Pie

*Makes 1 9" pie*

1 cup flour
⅔ cup brown sugar
1 Tbsp. vegetable shortening
1 egg

1 cup molasses
¾ cup boiling water
1 tsp. baking soda
1 9" unbaked pie shell

1. Mix flour, brown sugar and shortening. Reserve ½ cup of this crumb mixture for topping.
2. To the remaining crumb mixture add the egg, molasses, boiling water and soda. Spread mixture into unbaked pie shell.
3. Spread reserved crumbs over pie. Bake at 375° for 10 minutes. Reduce oven temperature to 350° and bake for 30 minutes longer.

*—Marian Sweigart, S. Clyde Weaver, Inc.*
*—Barbie King, Shreiner's Flowers*

# Wet Bottom Shoo-Fly Pie

*Makes 5 8" pies*

**Filling Ingredients:**
2 tsp. baking soda
3 cups boiling water
3 cups molasses
1 cup brown sugar
8 eggs
5 8" unbaked pie shells

**Crumb Ingredients:**
6 cups flour
2 cups brown sugar
1 tsp. baking soda
1½ cups shortening

1. Dissolve 2 tsp. soda in boiling water. Add remaining filling ingredients and mix well.
2. Mix all ingredients for crumbs. Beat 4 cups of crumbs into filling mixture. Save remaining crumbs.
3. Divide filling evenly into 5 unbaked pie shells. Use remaining crumbs to cover each pie.
4. Bake at 425° for 10 minutes. Reduce oven temperature to 350° and bake 45 minutes longer.

*—Sallie Y. Lapp, Sallie Y. Lapp*

# Sunday Pie

*Makes 1 9" pie*

3½-oz. pkg. lemon pudding
  and pie filling
1 pkg. unflavored gelatin
1 cup sugar
2¼ cups water
2 Tbsp. lemon juice

3 egg yolks
1 tsp. grated lemon rind
1 Tbsp. butter, melted
3 egg whites
1 cup whipped topping
1 9" baked pie shell

1. Combine pie filling mix, gelatin, sugar, ¼ cup water and lemon juice in saucepan. Blend in egg yolks and add remaining water. Cook and stir over medium heat until mixture comes to a full boil. Remove from heat.
2. Add lemon rind and butter.
3. Beat egg whites until peaks form. Gradually fold into hot pie filling. Cover with wax paper. Chill.
4. Blend whipped topping into chilled pie filling. Pour into pie shell.
5. Chill pie until set (about 3 hours). Garnish with remaining topping and lemon slices if desired.

Refreshing and delicious!

— *Viv Hunt, Viv's Varieties*

# Coconut Pie

*Makes 1 9" pie*

2 eggs, beaten
¾ cup sugar
1½ level Tbsp. flour
1½ Tbsp. milk
1½ cups milk

1 cup fresh coconut,
  shredded
1 tsp. vanilla
1 9" unbaked pie shell
½ cup coconut

1. Beat eggs and add sugar. Mix flour with 1½ Tbsp. milk to make a smooth paste. Beat flour mixture into egg and sugar mixture.
2. Heat 1½ cups milk to near boiling point. Add milk, coconut and vanilla to flour and egg mixture. Mix well.
3. Place into unbaked pie shell and spread more coconut over top of pie.
4. Bake at 400° for 15 minutes. Reduce oven temperature to 350° and bake 30 minutes longer or until pie is done.

— *Ruth L. Mellinger, C. H. Thomas and Son*

# Amish Pie

*Makes 2 9" pies*

2 cups sugar
1 cup flour
1 cup molasses
3 cups thick milk or
   buttermilk

2 eggs
1 tsp. baking soda
1 tsp. vanilla
½ cup coconut
2 9" unbaked pie shells

1. Mix all ingredients and pour into 2 unbaked pie shells.
2. Bake at 425° for 15 minutes. Reduce oven temperature to 350° and bake another 30 minutes or until done.

       *—Lois Thomas, C. H. Thomas and Son*

# Vanilla Pie

*Makes 4 8" pies*

*Pie Ingredients:*
1 cup sugar
1 cup molasses
3 cups water
1 heaping Tbsp. flour
1 egg, beaten
1 Tbsp. vanilla
4 8" unbaked pie shells

*Crumb-Topping Ingredients:*
2½ cups flour
1½ cups brown sugar
½ cup lard
1 tsp. baking soda
1 tsp. cream of tartar

1. Mix all pie ingredients and cook over medium heat until well mixed.
2. Pour into unbaked pie shells.
3. Mix all crumb ingredients. Spread over vanilla pie filling.
4. Bake at 350° for 40 minutes.

       *—Rebecca King, John R. Stoner Vegetables*

> **The best thing about working with my father, Chester Thomas, was the way he gave us responsibility. He did not order us around. Rather he made us responsible for certain jobs even when we were young boys.**
>       *—Ernie Thomas, C. H. Thomas and Sons*

# Pecan Pie

*Makes 1 8" pie*

| | |
|---|---|
| **3 eggs** | **½ tsp. vanilla** |
| **⅔ cup sugar** | **¼ tsp. salt** |
| **¾ cup King® syrup** | **1 cup pecan halves** |
| **4 Tbsp. butter, melted** | **1 8" unbaked pie shell** |

1. Beat eggs slightly. Add all other ingredients except pecans. Mix well.
2. Spread pecans in unbaked pie shell and pour mixture over them.
3. Bake at 400° for 10 minutes. Reduce oven temperature to 350° and bake for 25 more minutes.

Hint: If you see pie is getting too dark before it is finished or set, cover it for the last few minutes with foil or turn the oven off and let it set as oven cools.

My guests often comment that this pie is especially good because it is not terribly sweet.

—*Arlene Leaman, S. Clyde Weaver, Inc.*

# Frozen Yogurt Pie

**2 8-oz. containers fruit flavored yogurt**
**1 9-oz. container whipped topping**
**1 6-oz. graham cracker pie crust**

1. Use favorite graham cracker crust recipe.
2. Fold yogurt into whipped topping, blending well.
3. Spoon yogurt into crust. Freeze until firm (4 hours or overnight).
4. Before serving move to refrigerator at least 30 minutes or longer for softer texture.

Cool and light, this can be made with your favorite yogurt.

—*Joyce Fair, Utz's Potato Chips*

**Variations:**
   1. Garnish with any choice of topping.
   2. Fold diced fruit in with yogurt and whipped topping to give added texture.

◆

# Never Fail Pastry

*Makes 4 9" pie shells*

3 cups flour
1 tsp. salt
1 cup vegetable shortening

1 egg, beaten
¼ cup cold water
1 Tbsp. vinegar

1. Mix flour and salt. Cut in shortening.
2. Combine remaining ingredients and stir into shortening mixture. Knead until flour is thoroughly mixed into shortening and dough forms a ball.
3. With a rolling pin roll dough onto floured board to desired thickness and size.

*—Ethel Stoner, John R. Stoner Vegetables*

# Crumbs for Top of Pie

*Covers 1 9" pie*

¼ cup brown sugar
¼ cup white sugar
¾ cup flour
⅓ cup shortening (scant)

1. Mix sugar and flour together. Cut in shortening, mixing until crumbly.
2. Crumble over top of pie before baking.

*—Ethel Stoner, John R. Stoner Vegetables*

◆

# Chocolate Cake
# with Peanut Butter Icing

*Makes 12 – 16 servings*

**Cake Ingredients:**
1 tsp. baking powder
2 tsp. baking soda
2 cups all purpose flour
pinch salt (optional)
2 cups granulated sugar
¾ cup cocoa
2 eggs
½ cup vegetable oil
1 cup hot strong gourmét
  coffee
1 cup milk
2 tsp. vanilla

**Icing Ingredients:**
2 cups chunky peanut butter
¾ cup confectioner's sugar
1 tsp. butter, softened
1 Tbsp. milk

1. In a small bowl combine baking powder, baking soda, flour and salt (optional).
2. In a larger mixing bowl combine dry ingredients, sugar and cocoa. Beat in the eggs. Add oil, coffee, milk and vanilla. Batter should be thin and runny. Pour into a floured 9″ × 13″ cake pan.
3. Bake at 350° for 30 – 35 minutes. Do not overbake.
4. To prepare icing, mix peanut butter and confectioner's sugar on high speed until smooth. Add milk and butter to incorporate more smoothness.
5. Spread icing on cake after cake has cooled.

    The Haverstick clan has a sweet tooth. This cake is a sure dessert pleaser. I usually bake the cake the day before a family get-together and spread the icing just before leaving for the event.
          *— Lisa Mae Knight, Windows on Steinman Park*

# Chocolate Cake

*Makes 12–15 servings*

3 eggs
1¾ cups sugar
2¼ cups cake flour
¾ cup cocoa
2 tsp. baking soda

1½ tsp. salt
1 cup cooking oil
2 tsp. vanilla
1½ cups buttermilk or sour
  milk

1. Beat eggs and sugar in small bowl until thickened.
2. In large bowl sift together flour, cocoa, soda and salt. Mix oil and vanilla. Alternately add oil mixture and milk to dry ingredients.
3. Combine chocolate mixture with sugar mixture. Pour into two greased and floured 8″-square pans or one 9″ × 13″ pan.
4. Bake at 350° for 35 minutes.

**Hint:** 2 Tbsp. cornstarch per each cup of regular flour equals cake flour.

A friend passed this on to me as a constructive way to use up sour milk which collects from time to time.
— *Fannie S. Fisher, Tom's Flower Garden*

# Marble Cake

*Makes 12–14 servings*

¾ cup shortening
2 cups sugar
1½ cups milk or water
4 egg whites
3½ cups flour

½ tsp. salt
3 tsp. baking powder
3 tsp. vanilla
2 ozs. unsweetened chocolate
¼ tsp. baking soda

1. Cream shortening, sugar and 2 Tbsp. milk or water until light and fluffy. Add unbeaten egg whites to mixture one at a time, beating well after each addition.
2. Sift flour and measure it. Sift again with salt and baking powder. Add sifted dry ingredients alternately with remaining milk or water to creamed mixture. Add vanilla.
3. Divide batter into two equal parts.
4. Melt chocolate and combine with baking soda. Pour chocolate into one part batter and mix well.
5. Drop batter by large spoonfuls into a greased and floured 9″ × 13″ pan, alternating the white and chocolate batters until all used. Draw a knife through the batter to create marbling effect.
6. Bake at 350° for 40–45 minutes.

— *Nancy Geib, Nancy's Goodies*

◆

# Strawberry Shortcake

*Makes 10 – 12 servings*

| | |
|---|---|
| 2 eggs | ½ tsp. salt |
| 1 cup sugar | 2 tsp. baking powder |
| 2 Tbsp. butter or margarine, melted | 1 cup milk |
| 2½ cups flour | 1 tsp. vanilla |

1. Beat together eggs, sugar and melted butter. Add all remaining ingredients and beat until thoroughly blended.
2. Pour into two greased 8″ cake pans or one 9″ × 13″ pan.
3. Bake at 375° for 25 minutes. Serve warm with fresh strawberries and milk.

*— Rose Meck, Robert S. Meck*

# Orange Glazed Shortcake

*Makes 12 – 18 servings*

**Batter Ingredients:**
1¼ cups boiling water
1½ cups raisins
½ cup butter, softened
2 cups brown sugar
2 eggs
3 cups flour
1 tsp. baking soda
2 tsp. cinnamon
1 tsp. ground allspice

**Frosting Ingredients:**
3 cups confectioner's sugar
3 Tbsp. butter, softened
3 Tbsp. orance juice concentrate
2 Tbsp. cold water

1. Steam raisins in boiling water for 5 minutes.
2. Cream butter and sugar together. Add eggs and mix. Add undrained raisins and mix well.
3. Sift together dry ingredients and mix with batter. Do not over-mix. Batter should be thin. Pour mixture into two jelly roll pans. Spread to edge.
4. Bake at 350° for 12 – 15 minutes.
5. Mix all frosting ingredients and spread over shortcake while still warm.

*— Anna Mary Neff, S. Clyde Weaver, Inc.*

◆

# Blueberry Cake

*Makes 8 servings*

| | |
|---|---|
| 1 egg | 2 cups flour |
| 1 cup sugar | 1 tsp. baking powder |
| 3 Tbsp. butter, melted | pinch of salt |
| ½ cup milk | 1 pint fresh blueberries |

1. Cream together egg, sugar and butter. Add milk and mix well. Add flour, baking powder and salt and mix again.
2. Fold blueberries into this stiff batter and pour into a greased square baking dish.
3. Bake at 350° for about 40 minutes.

*—Marilyn Denlinger, Irwin S. Widders Produce*

# Fresh Apple Cake

*Makes 6–8 servings*

| | |
|---|---|
| 2 cups peeled apples, coarsely chopped | ½ tsp. nutmeg |
| | ½ tsp. allspice |
| 1 cup sugar | ½ cup vegetable oil |
| 1½ cups flour | 1 egg |
| 1 tsp. baking soda | ½ cup raisins |
| ½ tsp. salt | ½ cup walnuts, chopped |
| 1 tsp. cinnamon | |

1. Combine sugar and apples in large mixing bowl. Let stand 10 minutes.
2. Sift flour and add soda, salt, cinnamon, nutmeg and allspice.
3. Blend oil and egg into apple mixture. Add dry ingredients, stirring until blended. Fold in raisins and walnuts.
4. Spread evenly into greased 8″-square pan. Bake at 350° for 50–55 minutes. Cool for 10 minutes. Sprinkle with confectioner's sugar.

Easy to prepare and wonderful for family who loves apples.

*—Ruth B. White, Brenneman Farm*

◆

# Apple Cake

*Makes 8 servings*

¼ cup butter, melted
1 cup sugar
1 egg, beaten
1 cup flour
½ tsp. baking soda
½ tsp. baking powder

½ tsp. cinnamon
¼ tsp. salt
2 cups apples, chopped
½ cup walnuts, chopped
1 tsp. vanilla

1. Cream butter, sugar and egg together.
2. Mix all dry ingredients and add to sugar mixture. Fold in apples, walnuts and vanilla.
3. Bake at 350° for 35 minutes in an 8″-square baking dish.

— *Mrs. Martha Forry, John M. Markley Meats*

**Variation:**

Dust lightly with powdered sugar when cake is cooled to create a more festive appearance.

# Rhubarb Sour Cream Cake

*Makes 12 – 14 servings*

4 Tbsp. unsalted butter or
  margarine, softened
1½ cups brown sugar, firmly
  packed
1 egg
1 Tbsp. vanilla
2 – 3 cups flour

1 tsp. baking soda
1 tsp. salt
1 cup sour cream
4 cups red rhubarb, cut into
  ½ inch pieces
½ cup sugar
½ tsp. nutmeg

1. Cream butter and brown sugar until fluffy. Beat in egg and vanilla.
2. Sift flour with baking soda and salt. Add to mixture. Fold in sour cream and rhubarb. Spoon into greased 9″ × 13″ pan.
3. Mix sugar and nutmeg and sprinkle over batter.
4. Bake at 350° for 40 minutes.

— *Mrs. Jill Rauch, customer of Ethel Stoner*

◆

# Carrot Cake

*Makes 24 servings*

*Batter Ingredients:*
4 eggs
1 cup vegetable oil
2 cups sugar
2 cups flour
2 tsp. baking soda
2 tsp. cinnamon
1 tsp. salt
3 cups raw carrots, grated

*Frosting Ingredients:*
6 oz. cream cheese, softened
4 Tbsp. butter or margarine, softened
4 cups confectioner's sugar
1½ tsp. vanilla
½ tsp. maple flavoring

1. Beat eggs and add vegetable oil. Mix all dry ingredients and add to egg mixture. Fold carrots into mixture.
2. Pour into greased and floured 9″ × 13″ pan. Bake at 350° for 40–50 minutes. Cool.
3. To prepare frosting beat cream cheese and butter together. Add confectioner's sugar, vanilla and flavoring. Beat well and spread over cooled cake.

*—Joanne Mylin, Irwin S. Widders Produce*

# Best Pineapple Cake

*Makes 12–16 servings*

*Cake Ingredients:*
2 cups flour
2 cups granulated sugar
2 tsp. baking powder
2 eggs
1 tsp. vanilla
20-oz. can crushed pineapple
1 cup nuts, chopped

*Topping Ingredients:*
8-oz. pkg. cream cheese
8 Tbsp. margarine, softened
1½ cups confectioner's sugar
½ tsp. vanilla
½ cup nuts, chopped

1. Mix all dry ingredients for cake. Add eggs, vanilla and undrained pineapples. Blend well. Add nuts.
2. Pour into greased 9″ × 13″ pan. Bake at 350° for 45 minutes. Remove from oven and let cool before frosting.
3. To prepare topping mix cream cheese, margarine, sugar and vanilla and spread over cake. Sprinkle chopped nuts over topping.

*—Ethel Stoner, John R. Stoner Vegetables*

## THE CENTRAL MARKET, A CITY EDIFICE TO BE PROUD OF

**A fine example of the Romanesque Style of Architecture which Reflects Credit on the Architect and Contractor. Good Accomodations.**

The near completion of the new Central Market House, built by the City of Lancaster to take the place of the unsightly old structures that formerly stood in the rear of the City Hall, has induced us to publish today's full description of the beautiful new structure . . .

Of the several plans presented that of Mr. James H. Warner, formerly of London, England, but now a resident of our city, was the one adopted at the meeting of City Council held March 23. He was also engaged to superintend the building operations and the result is the possession by Lancaster of one of the finest market houses in the State . . . Rains have interfered greatly with the work and prevented it being carried forward as rapidly as it would have been had the weather been more favorable, but, nevertheless, the contractors have nearly completed the building at the specified time and the work has been well done. Material and workmanship have been of the best and the structure is one that will last many years. It is a market house of which our people may well feel proud, for it combines to a marked degree the properties of architectural beauty, durability, comfort and convenience, besides being so arranged as to secure the best sanitary conditions.

The plans for securing the best light and ventilation possible are admirable . . .

The lighting of the building is partly obtained from numerous large windows on all sides, raised above the side stall, but mainly from small dormer windows on all sides scattered all about the roof, the effect of this arrangement being very pleasing. The floor, which has a general, easy slope from east to west, is of concrete and is admirably adapted to secure cleanliness, as it can easily be flushed with water from plugs placed at convenient points. This fine even floor, so easily cleaned will leave no excuse for a dirty, ill smelling market, a subject of much universal complaint . . . The architect has confined himself principally to the south front in the design, and expenditure for ornament, as most of the other parts of the building are so surrounded by buildings as not to be much seen. This elevation shows a tower upon each corner and a gable in the centre . . .

The floor plan of the building shows an admirable arrangement of stalls and aisles, with entrances on all sides of the edifice. The truckers and farmers are placed in the centre of the market, the butchers being along the walls and the fish stall at the outside of the rear of the building . . . The stalls which will be in place within two weeks will all be constructed in the most approved modern style, all being of yellow pine.

The butchers' blocks will be of oak . . . there will be 100 farmers' and truckers' stalls, 72 butchers' and 20 fish stalls, 252 altogether.

The small streets about the building will be put in good condition as soon as possible, and in a little while our people will have one of the finest market houses in the State and all at a total of $26,500 . . . the only regret is that it does not occupy a site where it could be seen to its fullest advantage . . .

# Pineapple Zucchini Cake

*Makes 24 servings*

3 eggs
2 cups sugar
2 tsp. vanilla
1 cup cooking oil
2 cups zucchini, peeled and
  grated
3 cups flour

1 tsp. baking powder
1 tsp. baking soda
1 tsp. salt
½ cup crushed pineapple,
  not drained
1 cup raisins
1 cup nuts

*Cream Cheese Frosting Ingredients:*

2 cups confectioner's sugar
3-oz. pkg. cream cheese
¼ lb. margarine, softened

1. Beat eggs, sugar, vanilla and cooking oil until fluffy. Add zucchini, flour, baking powder, baking soda and salt.
2. Stir in pineapple, raisins and nuts and mix well.
3. Spoon into a greased 9″ × 13″ baking dish and bake at 350° for 1 hour, or make cupcakes and bake for 18–20 minutes.
4. Mix all frosting ingredients and frost cake or cupcakes.
                  *—Rachie Howard, customer of Irwin S. Widders Produce*

# Date Nut Cake

*Makes 12–14 servings*

2 cups dates, chopped
2 cups very warm water
2 tsp. baking soda
2 Tbsp. butter, softened
2 eggs

2 cups brown sugar
3 cups flour
2 tsp. vanilla
1 cup nuts, chopped

1. Dissolve soda in very warm water and pour over dates. Set aside.
2. Cream butter, eggs and sugar together. Add flour and vanilla.
3. Fold in nuts and date mixture.
4. Pour into 9″ × 13″ pan and bake at 375° for 25–30 minutes.
                  *—Fannie Esh, Frank Weaver Greenhouses*

◆

# Matrimony Cake

*Makes 12 servings*

*Batter Ingredients:*
3 cups quick oatmeal
2 cups flour
1¼ cups brown sugar
½ tsp. baking soda
pinch of salt
1 cup margarine, softened

*Filling Ingredients:*
1 lb. dates, chopped
1 cup white sugar
1½ cups water

1. To prepare batter mix all dry ingredients. Work margarine into dry ingredients. Put about ¾ of mixture into well-greased and floured 9″ × 13″ pan. Press down.
2. Mix all filling ingredients and boil until thickened. Spread over batter in pan.
3. Sprinkle remaining crumbs over date mixture.
4. Bake at 375° for 15–20 minutes or until lightly browned.

— *Laberta Minney, Shenk's Cheese Co.*

# Oatmeal Cake

*Makes 20 servings*

*Cake Ingredients:*
1 cup quick oatmeal
1½ cups boiling water
½ cup shortening
1 cup brown sugar, packed
1 cup white sugar
2 eggs
1⅓ cups flour
1 tsp. cinnamon
1 tsp. baking soda
½ tsp. salt
½ tsp. nutmeg
1 tsp. vanilla

*Topping Ingredients:*
½ cup margarine
½ cup brown sugar
½ cup milk
½ cup nuts, chopped
1 cup coconut

1. Pour boiling water over oatmeal and set aside.
2. Cream shortening and sugars until fluffy. Add eggs and beat well.
3. Mix all dry ingredients and add to batter. Add oatmeal and vanilla and mix well.
4. Pour into a greased and floured 9″ × 13″ pan and bake at 350° for 40–45 minutes.
5. To prepare topping melt margarine. Add sugar and milk and cream together. Bring mixture to a boil and cool slightly. Add nuts and coconut and spread over hot cake. Place under broiler until topping bubbles, watching carefully to prevent burning.

— *Deb Martin, Martin's Home-Baked Goods*

# Angel Food Cake

*Makes 10 – 12 servings*

1½ cups cake flour
1½ cups granulated sugar
1½ cups egg whites (10 – 12)
1¼ tsp. cream of tartar

¼ tsp. salt
¼ tsp. almond extract
1 tsp. vanilla extract

1. Sift flour and ½ cup sugar together four times. Set aside.
2. Beat egg whites until foamy. Add cream of tartar and salt. Beat until peaks form.
3. Add remaining sugar to egg whites, about 2 Tbsp. at a time. Add almond and vanilla extracts.
4. Fold flour into egg whites, about ¼ cup at a time. Fold in until no flour shows. Do not beat.
5. Spoon into an ungreased angel food cake pan and bake at 350° for about 40 minutes.

— *Mary King, Shreiner's Flowers*

# Feather Cake

*Makes 12 – 15 servings*

2 cups sugar
½ cup butter, softened
3 eggs

3 cups flour
2 tsp. baking powder
1 cup sweet milk

1. Cream sugar and butter. Add eggs and beat until well mixed.
2. Mix flour and baking powder. Alternately add flour and milk to mixture. Mix well.
3. Pour into two greased 8″ cake pans.
4. Bake at 350° for 35 – 40 minutes.

Great with chocolate icing!

— *Laberta Minney, Shenk's Cheese Co.*

◆

# Sponge Cake Receipt

*Original receipt from 1880's:*

1 lb. sugar                          10 eggs
½ lb. flour                          juice and rind of 1 lemon

*Recipe as you would make it today:*

10 eggs                              juice and rind of 1 lemon
2 cups sugar                         2 cups cake flour

1. Separate eggs. Beat yolks until thick and lemon colored. Gradually beat in sugar and add lemon juice and rind.
2. Beat egg whites until stiff. Fold egg whites into egg yolk mixture. Fold in the flour.
3. Turn into a greased and floured bundt pan. Bake at 350° for about 50 minutes.

This recipe was taken from a hand-written cookbook which I own. It was written by a lady from Strasburg. The book was written between 1872 and 1903. This is an appropriate recipe since it would have been used around the time when Central Market was built. In the 1800s, recipes were called receipts and, as you can see, most only listed ingredients. The mixing and baking was left to the skill of the cook. You were expected to know how to mix and bake cakes, cookies and breads.

— *Thomas L. Martin, Willow Valley Farms*

The mother of Charles Demuth used to shop at Central Market. Many of the beautiful fruits and vegetables which appear in his paintings were purchased from the produce stands of Lancaster County farmers.

— *Geraldine Alvarez, relative of R. P. Howry*

# Molasses Crumb Cake

*Makes 9 servings*

**Crumb Ingredients:**
1 cup sugar
½ cup shortening
2 cups flour
½ tsp. cinnamon
½ tsp. cloves
½ tsp. salt

**Batter Ingredients:**
1 tsp. baking soda
1 cup buttermilk or sour milk
4 Tbsp. baking molasses

1. Mix all crumb ingredients and save ¾ cup of crumbs.
2. To prepare batter pour milk over baking soda. Pour this mixture over molasses. Add all crumbs except the reserved ¾ cup and mix well.
3. Pour into greased and floured 9″ square cake pan. Sprinkle ¾ cup crumbs evenly over batter.
4. Bake at 350° for 25 minutes or until done.

This was my Grandmother Wooding's recipe.
> —*Barbara J. Weaver, D. M. Weaver and Sons, Inc.*

# Shoofly Cake

*Makes 15–20 servings*

4 cups flour
1 lb. dark brown sugar
1 cup butter or margarine, softened

1 cup molasses (King Syrup®)
2 cups boiling water
2 tsp. soda

1. Combine flour, sugar and butter. Work into fine crumbs. Reserve 1½ cups crumbs for topping.
2. Mix all remaining ingredients and the rest of the crumbs until batter is thin. Pour into greased and floured 9″ × 13″ pan. Sprinkle reserved crumbs on top.
3. Bake at 350° for 45 minutes.

> —*Helen E. Bitner, Bitners*

# Yum Yum Coffee Cake

*Makes 12 servings*

**Batter Ingredients:**
½ cup butter, softened
1 cup sugar
2 eggs
1 tsp. vanilla
1 cup sour cream
2 cups flour
1 tsp. baking soda
1 tsp. baking powder
½ tsp. salt

**Topping Ingredients:**
½ cup brown sugar
½ cup white sugar
1 tsp. cinnamon
1 cup nuts

1. Cream butter until soft. Add sugar and mix until fluffy.
2. Add eggs, one at a time, vanilla and sour cream, beating after each addition.
3. Sift flour, soda, baking powder and salt. Add dry ingredients to creamed mixture.
4. Spoon half of batter into a lightly greased 9″ × 13″ pan. Cover with half the topping. Add remaining batter and cover with remaining topping.
5. Bake at 325° for 40 minutes.

—*Mary E. Hess, Charles Hess*

Our business took off during the Depression. I think there were several reasons for this. People had time to shop because they were not working at all or at least not working 60-hour weeks. The market was a direct line between the producer and the consumer. It was the most economical place to shop. I always say that a recession is good for the public market.

—*Paul L. Neff, S. Clyde Weaver, Inc.*

# Cinnamon Flop Coffee Cake

*Makes two 9-inch cakes*

2 cups sugar
2 Tbsp. butter, softened
3 eggs
2 tsp. lemon extract
4 cups flour
4 tsp. baking powder
2 cups milk
2 tart apples, peeled and
   sliced thinly

1 tsp. cinnamon
½ cup brown sugar
1 cup sliced almonds
2 Tbsp. butter

1. Cream butter and sugar. Beat in eggs, one at a time. Beat mixture by hand until fluffy. Add lemon extract.
2. Sift flour, measure and combine with baking powder. Add dry ingredients alternately with milk into creamed mixture.
3. Divide mixture between two greased and floured 9-inch layer pans. Press apple slices on top. Sprinkle with almonds, cinnamon and brown sugar. Dot with butter.
4. Bake at 375° 30 minutes or until done. Serve warm or at room temperature.

The original recipe is from my maternal grandmother. I add apples, lemon and almonds because I enjoy the added flavors.
— *Cindy Cover, Marion Cheese*

# Yummy Cupcakes

*Makes 30 cupcakes*

**Batter Ingredients:**
2 cups sugar or less, as
   desired
3 cups flour
½ cup unsweetened cocoa
2 tsp. baking soda
2 Tbsp. vinegar
⅔ cup vegetable oil
2 cups water
2 tsp. vanilla

**Filling Ingredients:**
8-oz. pkg. cream cheese,
   softened
1 egg
½ cup sugar
dash of salt
12-oz. pkg. chocolate chips

1. Combine all batter ingredients and mix thoroughly.
2. To prepare filling combine cream cheese, egg, sugar and salt. Add chocolate chips and blend well.
3. Fill cupcake cups ½ full of batter. Top with 1 heaping tsp. filling.
4. Bake 15–20 minutes at 350°.
— *Donna Betancourt, Eisenberger's Baked Goods*

◆

# Banana Cupcakes

*Makes 24 – 30 cupcakes*

| | |
|---|---|
| ½ cup shortening | 2 cups flour |
| 1½ cups sugar | ½ tsp. salt |
| 2 eggs, beaten | 1 tsp. baking powder |
| 1 tsp. vanilla | ¼ cup sour milk |
| 1 cup ripe mashed bananas | ¾ tsp. baking soda |

1. Cream shortening and sugar together and beat until fluffy. Add beaten eggs, vanilla and mashed bananas and mix well.
2. Mix together flour, salt and baking powder. Mix together sour milk and baking soda. Alternately add flour mixture and sour milk mixture to shortening mixture. Mix thoroughly.
3. Fill greased muffin pans or cupcake cups ½ full.
4. Bake at 350° for 15 – 20 minutes.

Wonderful when topped with peanut butter icing and a few ground black walnuts.

— *Ruth Widders, Irwin S. Widders Produce*

# Ganache Icing

*Frosts 1 9″-square cake*

7½-oz. pkg. semi-sweet chocolate
¾ cup heavy cream
1½ Tbsp. butter, softened

1. Melt chocolate in double boiler, stirring constantly.
2. Bring cream to a boil. Stir hot cream into melted chocolate a little at a time. Make sure mixture stays smooth.
3. Stir in butter until completely melted. Let set overnight or at least 8 – 12 hours until stiff enough to use.

**Hint:** To coat cake with a thin layer, allow to cool only slightly (about one hour). Pour frosting over cake which is resting on a rack.

Very rich and very silky!

— *Peter Kovalec, Windows on Steinman Park*

# COOKIES

◆

# Pumpkin Cookies

*Makes 7 – 8 dozen cookies*

3 cups sugar
1 cup oil
3 cups cooked pumpkin
3 tsp. cinnamon
2 tsp. cloves
3 tsp. vanilla

6 cups flour, sifted
3 tsp. baking soda
3 tsp. baking powder
2 cups raisins
1 cup nuts (optional)

*Caramel Frosting:*
3 Tbsp. butter
4 tsp. milk
½ cup brown sugar
¾ tsp. vanilla
1 – 1¼ cups confectioner's
    sugar

1. Mix sugar, oil and cooked pumpkin. Slowly add spices, sifted flour, soda and baking powder. Mix thoroughly. Fold in raisins and nuts.
2. Drop on greased cookie sheets and bake at 375° 10 – 15 minutes. Do not overbake.
3. Remove from oven. Cool slightly and frost with caramel frosting.
4. To prepare frosting cook butter, milk, brown sugar and vanilla over low heat until mixture is smooth. Remove from heat and add confectioner's sugar. Stir until very smooth. Keep frosting warm and frost each tray of cookies as soon as it can be handled.

All you have to do is taste one. You will be hooked!
— *Ethel Stoner, John R. Stoner Vegetables*

My parents drove in from Mt. Nebo on every market day. I remember getting up at 4 a.m. I loved walking around the market looking at the food and occasionally buying something. My dad knew how much I liked a special type of waffle sold on market in those days. He bought me a waffle iron which I use to this day to make those waffles. I think they were called German waffles.
— *Miriam Hess, Frank Weaver Greenhouses*

◆

# Potato Chip Cookies

*Makes 3½ dozen cookies*

**1 lb. margarine or butter, softened**
**1 cup sugar**
**3½ cups flour**
**1 cup potato chips, crushed**
**1 tsp. vanilla**
**1 cup confectioner's sugar**

1. Mix shortening, sugar and flour.
2. Stir in potato chips and vanilla.
3. Chill overnight.
4. Roll into small balls (about 1 rounded teaspoon each) and flatten on cookie sheet with fork.
5. Bake at 350° for 15 minutes.
6. Lay out on paper towels or rack to drain excess shortening.
7. Sprinkle cookies with confectioner's sugar while still warm.

Visit Central Market and buy Utz's Potato Chips for this interesting cookie.

— *Customer of Joyce Fair, Utz's Potato Chips*

# Banana Cookies

*Makes 4 dozen cookies*

**½ cup margarine, softened**
**1 cup sugar**
**2 eggs**
**1 tsp. vanilla**

**2½ cups flour**
**2½ tsp. baking powder**
**½ tsp. salt**
**1 cup ripe mashed bananas**

1. Cream margarine and sugar until fluffy.
2. Add eggs, vanilla, flour, baking powder and salt.
3. Fold in mashed bananas.
4. Drop by teaspoonfuls onto greased cookie sheet and bake at 350° for 12 minutes.

Wonderfully tasty and moist cookies!

— *Ruth Widders, Irwin S. Widders Produce*

◆

# Molasses Cookies

*Makes 6 – 7 dozen cookies*

1½ cups lard or vegetable shortening, melted
1 cup granulated sugar
½ cup dark brown sugar
2 cups New Orleans® molasses, or substitute 1 cup table
    molasses plus 1 cup Black Strap® molasses
2 Tbsp. baking soda
½ cup boiling water
1 tsp. ginger
1 tsp. cinnamon
10 cups flour

1. Melt lard over low heat. Mix well with granulated and brown sugar. Add molasses and mix well.
2. Bring water to a boil and add soda to boiling water. Add to molasses mixture.
3. Add ginger and cinnamon to flour. Then add flour to molasses mixture and mix well.
4. Roll dough into balls and place on greased cookie sheet. Press down lightly with fork and sprinkle with granulated sugar.
5. Bake at 375° 10 – 15 minutes.

This recipe came from one of my husband's aunts at least 50 years ago.

*—Mrs. Aaron Z. King, Kauffman's Fruit Farm*

# Sugar Cookies

*Makes 6 dozen cookies*

7 Tbsp. margarine, softened
2 cups sugar
3 eggs, beaten
1 cup cultured sour cream
4 cups all purpose flour,
    sifted

1 tsp. baking soda
1 tsp. baking powder
¾ tsp. salt

1. Cream together margarine and sugar. Add beaten eggs and sour cream.
2. Sift together flour, soda, baking powder and salt and add to batter. Chill batter several hours or overnight.
3. Drop by teaspoonfuls onto greased cookie sheet and bake at 375° for 8 – 10 minutes.

*—Lois Thomas, C. H. Thomas and Son*

# Butter Pecan Cookies

*Makes 3 – 4 dozen cookies*

**2 Tbsp. butter, softened**
**½ cup brown sugar**
**1 cup pecans, chopped**
**½ cup butter, softened**
**1¼ cups brown sugar**

**2 cups flour**
**½ tsp. baking powder**
**1 egg**
**½ tsp. vanilla extract**

1. Combine 2 Tbsp. butter, ½ cup brown sugar and pecans. Mix until blended together. Set aside.
2. In large mixing bowl combine ½ cup butter, 1¼ cups brown sugar and all remaining ingredients. Blend well with mixer. Stir pecan mixture into this until evenly distributed.
3. Shape dough into walnut-sized balls and place on ungreased cookie sheet. Flatten balls slightly with the bottom of a glass which has been greased and dipped into flour.
4. Bake cookies at 375° for 8 – 10 minutes. Cool about 2 – 3 minutes before removing from cookie sheet.

*—Janice Kreider, Eisenberger's Baked Goods*

# Tea Cookies

*Makes 12 – 24 cookies*

**⅔ cup confectioner's sugar**
**½ cup shortening, softened**
**1 egg**
**1 tsp. lemon rind or vanilla or amaretto**
**1½ cups flour**

1. Whip confectioner's sugar, shortening and egg until they become light in color and very creamy. Add flavoring and stir. While stirring, gently sprinkle in the flour. Continue to fold in flour until well-mixed.
2. Drop batter by tablespoonfuls onto greased cookie sheet.
4. Bake at 325° 5 – 10 minutes or until peaks of dough just begin to toast.

Put cookies in the oven, then start your cup of coffee or tea for tasting the first cookies out of the oven!

*—Barbara J. Weaver, D. M. Weaver and Sons, Inc.*

# Ice Box Cookies

*Makes 3 dozen small cookies*

½ cup butter or
  shortening, softened
1 cup brown sugar
1 egg, beaten

2 cups flour
½ tsp. cream of tartar
1 tsp. baking soda
½ cup nuts, chopped

1. Mix all ingredients together and shape into log rolls, 1″ in diameter. Put into refrigerator and allow to stiffen. Slice rolls into thin pieces, ⅛ – ¼″ thick.
2. Place on greased cookie sheet and bake at 375° for 8 – 10 minutes.
— *Paul B. Martin, Spring Glen Farm Kitchen, Inc.*

# Raisin-Filled Cookies

*Makes 2 dozen cookies*

**Batter Ingredients:**
2 cups light brown sugar
1 cup butter or margarine,
  softened
3 eggs
4 cups flour
1 tsp. baking soda
1 tsp. vanilla

**Filling Ingredients:**
1 cup raisins
1 cup light brown sugar
1 cup water
2 Tbsp. flour

1. Mix all batter ingredients. Chill until dough is stiff enough to roll.
2. Mix together all filling ingredients and bring to a boil. Cook until thickened. Let filling cool.
3. Roll out dough to ⅛″ thickness. Cut out rounds of dough with a cookie cutter and lay 1″ apart on greased cookie sheet. Top each with 1 tsp. filling. Cover with another round of dough. Then pinch edges together to prevent filling from cooking out.
4. Bake at 375° for 10 – 15 minutes.

This was my mother's favorite cookie recipe. She was Florence Heiney. She and her husband Samuel Heiney had a stand on Central Market for 25 years.
— *Miriam M. Hess, Frank Weaver Greenhouses*

# Mincemeat-Filled Cookies

*Makes 5 – 6 dozen cookies*

1 cup shortening, softened
2 cups brown sugar, packed
3 eggs
½ cup water
1 tsp. vanilla

3½ cups flour, sifted
½ tsp. salt
1 tsp. baking soda
⅛ tsp. cinnamon
1½ cups mincemeat

1. Cream together shortening, brown sugar and eggs. Stir in water and vanilla.
2. Sift together flour, salt, soda and cinnamon. Stir into batter. Drop by teaspoonfuls onto ungreased cookie sheet. Put about 1 tsp. mincemeat on dough. Cover mincemeat with another teaspoon dough.
3. Bake at 375° for 10 – 12 minutes or until lightly browned.

*— Paul B. Martin, Spring Glen Farm Kitchen, Inc.*

# Brownies

*Makes 24 brownies*

4 squares cooking chocolate
1 cup butter
4 eggs, beaten
1 tsp. baking powder
2 cups sugar

2 Tbsp. vanilla
dash of salt
1 cup flour
2 cups pecans or walnuts

1. Melt chocolate and butter in saucepan.
2. Remove from stove. Add all other ingredients. Stir well until blended. Pour into 9″ × 13″ baking pan.
3. Bake 20 minutes at 350°.

Moist and chewy!

*— Frances Kiefer, Kiefer's Meats & Cheese*

◆──────────────────────────────

# White Brownies

*Makes 35 brownies*

**Brownie Ingredients:**

¾ cup butter, melted
½ cup brown sugar
½ cup white sugar
3 egg yolks

1 tsp. vanilla
1 tsp. baking powder
2 cups flour
¼ tsp. salt

**Topping Ingredients:**
3 egg whites
1 cup brown sugar
½ cup nuts, chopped
½ cup chocolate chips

1. Thoroughly mix all ingredients for the brownie mixture. Spread batter in a 12″ × 17″ pan.
2. Beat egg whites until stiff. Add brown sugar. Spread this mixture over brownies.
3. Sprinkle with nuts and chocolate chips.
4. Bake at 350° for 35–40 minutes.

*—Mary Ellen Speicher, Sallie Y. Lapp*

# Chocolate Chip Squares

*Makes 20–24 servings*

⅔ cup shortening
2¼ cups brown sugar
3 eggs
2¼ cups flour

2½ tsp. baking powder
½ tsp. salt
12-oz. pkg. chocolate chips
1 tsp. vanilla

1. Cream shortening and sugar. Add eggs.
2. Combine flour with baking powder and salt. Mix slowly into creamed mixture. Add chocolate chips and vanilla.
3. Spread in greased 9″ × 13″ pan.
4. Bake 30 minutes at 350°. Cut while still warm.

*—Judith E. Martin, Paul L. Sensenig and Sons*

# Marble Squares

*Makes 4 dozen squares*

*Batter Ingredients:*
¾ cup water
1 to 1½ oz. unsweetened
　chocolate squares
½ cup butter or margarine
2 cups flour
2 cups granulated sugar

2 eggs
½ cup sour cream
1 tsp. baking soda
½ tsp. salt
1 cup semi-sweet chocolate
　chips

*Topping Ingredients:*
8-oz. pkg. cream cheese,
　softened
⅓ cup sugar
1 egg

1. Mix topping by combining softened cream cheese and sugar until well blended. Add egg and mix well until smooth. Set aside.
2. Combine water, unsweetened squares and butter or margarine in saucepan. Bring to boil. Remove from heat. Combine flour and sugar and stir into mixture. Add eggs, sour cream, baking soda and salt and mix well.
3. Pour into greased and floured 10″ × 15″ jelly roll pan. Spoon cheese topping over chocolate batter. Cut through batter several times for marbled effect. Sprinkle with chocolate chips.
4. Bake at 375° for 25–30 minutes or until toothpick inserted in center comes out clean.
5. Cool and cut into squares before serving.

Soft, delicious brownie!

—*Joyce Deiter, Eisenberger's Baked Goods*

◆

# Magic Cookie Bars

*Makes 36 cookies*

½ cup butter
1½ cups graham cracker crumbs
14-oz. can sweetened condensed milk
6-oz. pkg. semi-sweet chocolate chips
3½-oz. can flaked coconut
1 cup nuts, chopped

1. Melt butter in 8″ × 12″ baking pan. Sprinkle cracker crumbs over butter. Pour condensed milk evenly over crumbs.
2. Mix together chocolate chips, coconut and nuts, then sprinkle evenly over mixture.
3. Bake at 350° for 25–30 minutes.

— *Ruth Ann Kauffman, Sallie Y. Lapp*

# Sand Tarts

*Makes 6 dozen cookies*

*Cookie Ingredients:*
1½ cups sugar
½ lb. butter, melted
3 eggs, beaten
4 cups flour

2 tsp. cream of tartar
1 tsp. baking soda
1 tsp. vanilla

*Topping Ingredients:*
3 eggs, beaten
2–3 tsp. cinnamon
2–3 cups chopped peanuts

1. Cream together sugar and melted butter. Add beaten eggs.
2. Sift together flour, cream of tartar and baking soda. Add to batter. Add vanilla and mix well. Chill until stiff.
3. Roll out batter in a thin layer and cut out sand tarts into any shape desired. Place on greased cookie sheet. Spread small amount of beaten egg on each cookie and top with cinnamon and chopped peanuts.
4. Bake at 300° for 10–12 minutes.

This recipe was handed down from my great-grandmother and is a favorite family cookie.

— *Helen Thomas, Helen Thomas Produce*

◆

# Nellie Blyths

*Makes 10 dozen cookies*

4 eggs
2 cups granulated sugar
2 cups buttermilk
2 tsp. baking soda

7 cups flour
2–3 cups shortening
2 cups confectioner's sugar

1. Mix together eggs, granulated sugar, buttermilk, baking soda and flour.
2. Drop by scant teaspoonfuls into hot lard or shortening. Deep fry until light brown.
3. Drain in colander.
4. Shake in a bag of confectioner's sugar and serve.

These little desserts are best eaten when they are freshly made and still warm. If preparing to serve later let cool before dusting with confectioner's sugar.

*— Mary E. Hess, Charles Hess*

# English Lemon Tarts

*Makes 4 dozen tarts*

*Pastry Ingredients:*
2 cups flour
½ cup sugar
grated rind of 1 lemon
¾ cup butter, softened
3 egg yolks

*Lemon Curd Filling Ingredients:*
5 eggs
2 cups sugar
½ cup plus 2 Tbsp. butter, melted
grated rind and juice of 2 lemons

1. Mix flour, sugar and rind of one lemon in food processor. Cut in butter and add egg yolks one at a time. Mix until dough clings together.
2. Roll pastry until it is ⅛-inch thick. Fit pastry into greased tart shells. Bake shells at 375° for 12 minutes. Cool before filling.
3. In top of double boiler beat eggs and add sugar gradually. Add remaining ingredients and mix well. Cook over hot water until thick. Chill.
4. Using pastry bag or spoon, fill tarts with lemon curd. Sift confectioner's sugar over top and garnish with candied violets.

Great for an afternoon tea!

*— Jackie Parker, The Goodie Shoppe*

◆

# Hermits

*Makes 5 dozen cookies*

1 cup shortening (half
   butter), softened
2 cups brown sugar
2 eggs
2⅔ cups flour
½ tsp. salt
2 tsp. baking powder
½ tsp. baking soda

½ tsp. cinnamon
½ tsp. cloves
½ tsp. nutmeg
⅓ cup milk
⅔ cup raisins, chopped
⅔ cup nuts, chopped

1. Cream shortening and sugar together. Add eggs and beat until
fluffy.
2. Sift flour. Measure and add salt, soda, baking powder and spices
to flour. Sift again.
3. Add dry ingredients alternately with milk to shortening mixture.
Beat after each addition. Add chopped nuts and raisins and blend
into mixture.
4. Drop by teaspoonfuls onto greased baking sheet, placing about
2 inches apart.
5. Bake at 350° for 12–15 minutes.

                    *—Esther Eisenberger, Eisenberger's Baked Goods*

# DESSERTS
## AND
# CANDIES

◆

# Espresso Mousse

*Makes 10 – 12 servings*

**Mousse Ingredients:**
6 egg yolks
½ cup sugar
1½ cups espresso coffee
2 pkgs. unflavored gelatin
½ cup cold water
1½ pints heavy cream

**Sauce Ingredients:**
⅔ cup sugar
1 cup espresso, heated
1 Tbsp. arrowroot
1 Tbsp. cognac

1. Beat egg yolks with ½ cup sugar. Beat in coffee and cook over low heat, stirring constantly, until mixture forms a thin custard.
2. Remove from heat. Soften gelatin in cold water and blend thoroughly into custard. Let cool.
3. Whip cream and fold into the cooled custard.
4. Rinse a 2-quart mold with cold water, scrape the mousse into it and chill overnight. Cover with plastic wrap.
5. Dissolve ⅔ cup sugar in hot coffee. Mix arrowroot to thin paste with cold water and stir into the espresso. Cook, stirring constantly, until clear and thickened. Add cognac. Chill, covered with plastic wrap.
6. Unmold mousse and top with sauce and shaved chocolate, if desired.

Light as a cloud, this lovely rich dessert uses French roast espresso beans in a new way!

— *Regine Ibold, The Spice Stand*

My earliest memory of the market relates to the wife of a local doctor who used to shop on market. She and my mother were very close friends, and she would always marvel about how well-behaved Mother's children were. She gave me many special gifts including silver dollars on my birthday, a tea set and a German-made doll which my sister and I wore out because we played with it so much.

— *Viv Hunt, Viv's Varieties*

◆

# Spanish Cream

*Makes 8 – 10 servings*

2 pkgs. unflavored gelatin
3 cups milk
½ cup sugar
3 eggs, separated

¼ tsp. salt
1 tsp. vanilla
fresh fruit

1. Dissolve gelatin in cold milk. Add sugar, beaten egg yolks, salt and vanilla. Mix over low heat, stirring constantly. Immediately, when mixture starts to boil, remove from heat.
2. Beat egg whites until stiff and gently fold into mixture. Do not cook after adding egg whites. Pour into mold immediately.
3. Unmold and garnish around the edges with alternating slices of bananas and strawberries, or fill center of mold with raspberries, pineapples, peaches or apricots.

This easy light dessert came from my sister-in-law.
— *Anna Marie Groff, Ruth S. Nolt*

# Broken Glass Dessert

*Makes 16 servings*

½ cup sugar
½ cup butter, melted
24 whole graham crackers, crushed
3-oz. pkg. lemon gelatin
1½ cups hot water
3-oz. pkg. lime gelatin
1½ cups hot water

3-oz. pkg. strawberry gelatin
1½ cups water
3-oz. pkg. unflavored gelatin
¼ cup cold water
1 cup hot pineapple juice
1 pint whipping cream, whipped

1. Combine sugar, butter and the crushed graham crackers.
2. Place half of mixture in bottom of 9″ × 13″ pan.
3. Dissolve each package of flavored gelatin in 1½ cups hot water. Pour each into its own flat pan. Allow each to set until firm. Cut each gelatin into small squares. Gently stir the lemon, lime and strawberry squares together. Set aside.
4. Dissolve unflavored gelatin in cold water. Add hot pineapple juice. Cool mixture until it has syrupy consistency. Fold whipped cream and gelatin into the flavored gelatin squares and place in graham cracker crust. Sprinkle remaining crumbs over top and serve.

— *Charles Hess*

# Graham Cracker Fluff

*Makes 6 – 8 servings*

| | |
|---|---|
| 2 egg yolks | 1 tsp. vanilla |
| ½ cup sugar | 1 cup heavy cream |
| ⅔ cup milk | 3 Tbsp. butter, melted |
| 1 pkg. unflavored gelatin | 3 Tbsp. sugar |
| ½ cup cold water | 12 graham crackers, crushed |
| 2 egg whites, stiffly beaten | |

1. Beat egg yolks and add sugar. Add milk and cook in top of double boiler until slightly thickened.
2. Soak gelatin in cold water.
3. Pour hot mixture over softened gelatin. Stir until smooth. Chill until slightly thickened.
4. Add egg whites, vanilla and heavy cream to chilled mixture.
5. Combine melted butter, sugar and cracker crumbs to make crumbs. Sprinkle half of crumbs into bottom of serving dish. Spread chilled mixture over crumbs. Sprinkle remaining crumbs over top. Chill in refrigerator until set.

*— Mrs. Martha Forry, John M. Markley Meats*


# Butterscotch Supreme

*Makes 15 servings*

*First Layer:*
1½ cups flour
12 Tbsp. butter, melted
¾ cup walnuts, chopped

*Second Layer:*
8-oz. pkg. cream cheese, softened
1 cup confectioner's sugar
1 cup whipped topping

*Third Layer:*
2 pkgs. butterscotch pudding
3 cups milk
1 tsp. vanilla

*Fourth Layer:*
2 cups whipped topping
½ cup walnuts, chopped

1. Mix together all ingredients for first layer. Press into 9″ × 13″ pan and bake at 350° for 15 minutes. Cool.
2. Beat together all ingredients for second layer. Pour onto cooled first layer.
3. Mix together all ingredients for third layer. Pour over second layer.
4. Cover with whipped topping and sprinkle with chopped walnuts.
5. Chill before serving.

*— Mrs. Robert Funk, Funk Brothers, Inc.*

**Variation:**
Use any flavor pudding you wish.

# Pumpkin Custard

*Makes 6 servings*

| | |
|---|---|
| 2 cups mashed pumpkin | ½ tsp. cinnamon |
| ⅔ cup granulated sugar | ½ tsp. cloves |
| 1 Tbsp. flour | 2 eggs |
| ½ tsp. salt | 1 cup milk |
| ½ tsp. ginger | |

1. Combine all ingredients and mix well.
2. Pour into baking dish and bake at 350° about 35–40 minutes or until mixture thickens.

*—Mary K. Brieghner, Rudolph Breighner*

**Variation:**
Add vanilla and ½ cup coconut instead of spices.

# Pumpkin Roll

*Makes 8–10 servings*

**Pumpkin Roll Ingredients:**
3 eggs
1 cup sugar
⅔ cup Pumpkin Delight
¾ cup flour
1 tsp. baking soda
2 tsp. cinnamon

**Filling Ingredients:**
1 cup confectioner's sugar
8-oz. pkg. cream cheese, softened
4 Tbsp. butter
½ tsp. vanilla

1. Beat eggs for 5 minutes. Add all other pumpkin roll ingredients and mix well. Spread mixture into a generously greased and floured jelly roll pan.
2. Bake at 350° 15–20 minutes. Cool about 5 minutes.
3. Dust two paper towels with confectioner's sugar and gently lift cake from pan onto paper towels. Cool 5 more minutes and roll cake (paper towels and all). Let stand ½ hour.
4. Beat together all filling ingredients until smooth.
5. Unroll cake and spread with filling. Reroll cake without paper towels and refrigerate until firm.

Pumpkin Delight is a special mixture made by Shenk's Cheese Co. It may be purchased from our stand on Central Market.

*—Debbie Buhay, Shenk's Cheese Co.*

**Variation:**
If unable to purchase Pumpkin Delight, mix 1 pint pumpkin, ½ cup brown sugar and ¼ cup granulated sugar. Use ⅔ cup of this mixture for above recipe.

# Baked Apples

*Makes 4 servings*

**4 Granny Smith (or another tart variety) apples**
**2 tsp. cinnamon**
**¼ cup brown sugar**
**¼ cup raisins**
**8 apricots, chopped**
**¼ cup brandy or Grand Marnier®, heated slightly**
**⅛ cup butter, melted**
**1 tsp. nutmeg**

1. Combine cinnamon, brown sugar, raisins and apricots to make filling.
2. Core apples. Stuff apples with filling. Place in greased baking dish.
3. Combine remaining ingredients and pour over apples.
4. Bake at 350° for 40 minutes.

*—Kathleen Pianka, Marion Cheese*

# Apple Dumplings

*Makes 6 servings*

**Batter Ingredients:**
**2 cups flour**
**2½ tsp. baking powder**
**½ tsp. salt**
**⅔ cup shortening**
**¼ cup milk**

**Sauce Ingredients:**
**2 cups brown sugar**
**¼ tsp. cinnamon**
**2 cups water**
**¼ cup butter, softened**

**6 baking apples**
**enough sugar to fill centers of 6 apples**
**cinnamon**

1. Pare apples and slice in half. Fill centers with sugar and sprinkle with cinnamon. Put apples back together.
2. Make pastry by sifting flour, baking powder and salt. Cut in shortening and add milk. Roll dough as for pastry shell and cut into 6 squares. Place an apple on each square and wrap pastry around the apple. Place apples into a greased baking pan.
3. To make sauce, combine sugar, cinnamon and water. Cook 5 minutes. Remove from heat and add butter. Mix well. Pour sauce over the apple dumplings.
4. Bake at 375° for 40−45 minutes. Serve hot with milk.

*—Susie Beiler, Kauffman's Fruit Farm*

# Quick Apple Cobbler

*Makes 8 servings*

**Batter Ingredients:**
1 cup sugar
1 cup flour
2 tsp. baking powder
1 cup milk
½ tsp. salt
½ tsp. cinnamon

**Other Ingredients:**
8 Tbsp. margarine or butter
4 cups apples, diced

1. Mix all ingredients for batter. Set aside.
2. Melt margarine in 7″ × 12″ baking dish. Pour batter over melted margarine. Do not stir.
3. Pour apples over batter without stirring. Bake at 375° for 40 minutes.
4. Serve warm with milk or vanilla ice cream.

—*Ruth Thomas, Helen Thomas Produce*

**Variation:**
Substitute any fruit which is in season.

# Gourmet Apple Crisp

*Makes 6 servings*

9 fresh apples
1 cup flour
1 cup sugar
1 tsp. baking powder
pinch of salt

1 egg
4 Tbsp. butter or margarine
gourmet cinnamon
dash of cardamom

1. Cut apples into a greased 7″ × 11″ baking dish.
2. Mix flour, sugar, baking powder and salt. Break egg into mixture and continue to mix with your hands.
3. Pour mixture over apples.
4. Melt butter and pour over apples. Liberally sprinkle the mixture with gourmet cinnamon. Add a dash of cardamom for a slightly different flavor.
5. Bake at 350° for 50 minutes.

A family favorite for years!

—*Brad Loercher, Parsley Porch*

◆

# Rhubarb Pudding

*Makes 6 servings*

2 egg yolks
½ cup sugar
2 cups milk
2 cups bread, cubed

2 cups rhubarb, cut-up
2 Tbsp. butter
2 egg whites plus 2 Tbsp.
    sugar

1. Beat egg yolks. Add sugar, milk and bread cubes and mix well. Fold in rhubarb.
2. Put in casserole dish and dot with butter. Bake at 350° until knife comes out clean when inserted in middle of casserole (about 30–45 minutes).
3. Prepare a meringue by beating egg whites until stiff. Fold in sugar. Spread over casserole and return to oven to brown meringue.

This old receipt came from my home. We used it as a dessert.
— *Ruth Eshleman, Givant's Bakery*

# Rhubarb Crunch

*Makes 6–8 servings*

*Batter Ingredients:*
1 quart rhubarb, cut in
    1"-pieces
¾ cup granulated sugar
2 Tbsp. flour
1 tsp. cinnamon
⅛ tsp. salt

*Topping Ingredients:*
¾ cup oatmeal
¾ cup brown sugar
¼ cup butter, melted

1. Combine all batter ingredients. Spoon into bottom of greased 9"-square baking dish.
2. Combine oatmeal, brown sugar and butter. Sprinkle over rhubarb and pat down evenly.
3. Bake at 375° about 40 minutes.
4. Serve warm with milk or whipped cream.
— *Helen Craul, S. Clyde Weaver, Inc.*

# Orange Rhubarb

*Makes 10 – 12 servings*

4 cups rhubarb, chopped
½ cup water
1 cup sugar
3-oz. pkg. orange gelatin
1 can mandarin oranges

1. Boil rhubarb in water until it is soft (about 10 minutes). Add sugar and gelatin. Stir in oranges and continue stirring until gelatin is completely dissolved.
2. Cool until thickened and serve.

*—Mrs. Dorothy Martin, Martin's Home-Baked Goods*

# Rhubarb Sauce

*Makes 8 – 10 servings*

6 – 8 cups rhubarb
1 cup water
1½ – 2 cups sugar
2 – 3 Tbsp. minute tapioca

1. Wash rhubarb and cut into 1-inch pieces.
2. Put in saucepan with water and sugar and bring to a boil. Simmer until tender.
3. Add tapioca and stir until well mixed. Simmer an additional 5 minutes.
4. Cool and serve.

*—Ethel Stoner, John R. Stoner Vegetables*

**Variation:**
Substitute 3-oz. pkg. strawberry gelatin for tapioca.

---

Why was it acceptable for women to work on market? I think there were several reasons. First of all, it was only a part-time job. I would have felt badly about hiring a mother of young children to work full-time. Also many mothers took their children along to market. My mother took me when I was only six weeks old.

*—Anna Mary Neff, S. Clyde Weaver, Inc.*

◆

# Rhubarb Tapioca Pudding

*Makes 6 – 8 servings*

2 cups rhubarb pieces
2 cups water
¼ tsp. salt
1 cup sugar (or less, as desired)
¼ cup quick-cooking tapioca
8-oz. can crushed pineapple, drained, or 1 cup fresh
strawberries
1 cup whipping cream (whipped)

1. Combine rhubarb, water, salt, sugar and tapioca in saucepan. Cook over medium heat until mixture comes to a full boil, stirring constantly. Remove from heat.
2. Add crushed pineapple or strawberries and chill.
3. Top with whipped topping.

I like to make this in the microwave, stirring several times.
— *Ruth Widders, Irwin S. Widders Produce*

# Apple Tapioca

*Makes 4 – 6 servings*

⅓ cup tapioca
1 cup brown sugar, packed
4 cups apples
2 cups water
1 Tbsp. lemon juice
2 Tbsp. butter, softened
½ tsp. cinnamon
½ tsp. salt

1. Peel and chop apples.
2. Mix all ingredients together and let stand 5 minutes.
3. Over medium heat bring to a boil, stirring frequently.
4. Simmer until apples are tender (about 12 minutes).
— *Mrs. Dorothy Martin, Martin's Home-Baked Goods*

# Strawberry Tapioca

*Makes 6 servings*

**2 cups water**
**⅓ cup tapioca**
**½ cup sugar**
**2 cups fresh or frozen strawberries, crushed**
**1 cup whipped topping**

1. Boil water, tapioca and sugar until mixture begins to thicken. Remove from stove.
2. Add strawberries. Cool.
3. Serve with whipped topping.

— *Lois Thomas, C. H. Thomas and Son*

**Variation:**
Substitute ¼ cup lemon juice and rind from 2 lemons in place of 2 cups strawberries.

— *Helen Thomas, Helen Thomas Produce*

# Caramel Pudding

*Makes 6 servings*

**4 Tbsp. butter**
**4 cups milk**
**1 cup brown sugar**
**¼ tsp. salt**
**⅔ cup flour**
**2 tsp. vanilla**

1. Melt butter in large pan over low heat. Add milk and heat until milk is scalding.
2. Add sugar, salt and flour and cook until thickened. Remove from heat.
3. Stir in vanilla and cool overnight.
4. Serve with whipped cream topping, if desired.

A delicious family favorite.

— *Joyce Deiter, Eisenberger's Baked Goods*

# The
# Other Markets
## in
# Lancaster

The Central Market is now the only farmers' market in Lancaster; however, there were at least eight other markets that once operated within the city. Central Market has by far the longest history; only two other city markets lasted more than ninety years. Three Lancaster markets endured for less than 40 years. From 1882 to 1965 there were at least five farmers' markets operating simultaneously within Lancaster. The high point was between 1907 and 1918 when there were seven markets in the city. It was not uncommon for standholders to sell at several different markets on different days of the week.

**The Curb Market.** This street market existed from before 1818 to 1927. More detail is given on page 64.

**The Northern Market** was located on the northwest corner of Queen and Walnut Streets. Built in 1872, it was the first of the large market houses. The building measured 80 feet by 240 feet and contained 250 stalls. The relatively new market building suffered a great tragedy in 1883, when the roof collapsed from the weight of snow. When the market closed in 1953, there were only 15 occupied stands. The building was demolished in 1958.

**The Eastern Market** was built in 1882 at the southeast corner of King and Shippen Streets. It had about 200 stalls. The unique Second-Empire-style architecture featured towers which could be viewed over a large part of the city. The market closed in 1918. The building has been renovated and is now used for offices.

**The Western Market** occupied the southeast corner of Orange and Pine Streets. It was built in 1882 and contained about 180 stalls. Like the Eastern Market it enjoyed a rather brief existence and closed about 1920. The building still survives, but the second floor was destroyed by fire in 1942 (it was then being used as a roller skating rink).

**The Southern Market** was built in the elaborate Queen Anne style in 1888 at the southwest corner of Queen and Vine Streets. It survived until 1986, but from the 1950s on it suffered a dwindling trade. The building is now used by the Lancaster Chamber of Commerce.

**The Fulton Market,** located east of Frederick Street between Plum and Hand Streets in the northeastern part of town, was rather detached from the other Lancaster markets. The 1907 building originally had 150 standholders. When the market closed in 1971 there were only six stands. The building has been occupied by several different businesses.

**The Arcade Market** began in 1927 in the block between Orange and Marion Streets and Prince and Market Streets. The farmer's market continued until 1965; the entire building was demolished in 1969. The Prince Street parking garage now occupies the site.

**The West End Market,** the smallest and most recent of the markets, began in 1954 in a building that had been a car dealership. The building at the corner of Lemon and Mary Streets ceased to be a farmers' market in 1985 but is still occupied by a grocery store.

# Grape Nut Pudding

*Makes 6 servings*

½ cup brown sugar
⅛ tsp. salt
1 Tbsp. cornstarch
1 egg, beaten
½ cup grapenuts

2 cups milk
½ cup raisins
⅓ cup nuts, chopped
1 tsp. vanilla

1. Combine brown sugar, salt and cornstarch. Blend the beaten egg into dry mixture. Add grapenuts and milk and beat thoroughly.
2. Dust raisins and chopped nuts with flour and fold into mixture. Add vanilla.
3. Pour into greased 7″ × 11″ baking dish and bake at 350° for about 1 hour or until firm.

*—Joyce Fair, Utz's Potato Chips*

# Christmas Plum Pudding

*Makes 8–10 servings*

*Pudding Ingredients:*
1 cup ground suet (beef)
1 cup raisins
½ cup nuts, chopped
½ cup dried currants
⅔ cup milk
1 egg
1 scant cup sugar
1 cup flour
1 tsp. baking soda
½ tsp. cinnamon
½ tsp. nutmeg

*Sauce Ingredients:*
1 cup water
½ cup sugar
1 Tbsp. cornstarch
1 Tbsp. butter
pinch of salt
1 tsp. vanilla

1. Mix all pudding ingredients thoroughly. Pour into 2-quart casserole. Cover casserole and set into a 9″ × 13″ pan. Pour as much water as possible into the 9″ × 13″ pan. Bake at 300° for 2 hours. Check occasionally to make sure pan has not dried. Add water if needed.
2. Mix all sauce ingredients except vanilla. Bring to a boil and cook until thickened.
3. Serve warm sauce over warm pudding.

*—Anna Mary Neff, S. Clyde Weaver, Inc.*

◆

# Nut Pudding

*Makes 10 – 12 servings*

| | |
|---|---|
| 1 quart milk | 3 eggs, separated |
| 2 cups bread crumbs | ½ tsp. nutmeg (optional) |
| 1 cup sugar | 1 cup walnuts, chopped |

1. Mix milk with bread crumbs and cook, bringing to a boil.
2. Mix sugar, egg yolks and nutmeg, if desired. Add to bread mixture. Remove from heat.
3. Add walnuts to mixture and mix well.
4. Beat egg whites until stiff and spread over bread mixture. Bake at 400° for about 8 – 10 minutes or until egg whites brown.

This old recipe is a real conversation piece.

— *Grace E. Baker, S. Clyde Weaver, Inc.*

# Bread Pudding

*Makes 12 – 14 servings*

| | |
|---|---|
| 1 loaf bread | 2¾ cups sugar |
| 1½ quarts milk | 1 tsp. cinnamon |
| 10 eggs, beaten | 1 tsp. vanilla |

1. Break bread into mixing bowl. Pour half of milk over bread and fold together.
2. Spoon into greased 9″ × 13″ baking dish.
3. Mix remaining milk with eggs, sugar, cinnamon and vanilla. Mix well and pour over bread mixture using a spatula to push mixture down on bread.
4. Bake 1½ hours at 325°.

— *Willow Valley Farms*

# Cracker Pudding

*Makes 8 – 10 servings*

| | |
|---|---|
| 1 quart milk | ¾ cup coconut, grated |
| 2 egg yolks | 1 tsp. vanilla |
| ¾ cup sugar | 2 egg whites |
| 1 cup crumbled saltine crackers | ½ cup sugar |

1. Scald milk in a saucepan. Add egg yolks, ¾ cup sugar, cracker crumbs and coconut. Mix well, cooking and stirring constantly until thickened. Remove from heat and stir in vanilla.

2. Pour into a baking dish.

3. Beat egg whites until stiff and add ½ cup sugar to make a meringue. Spread over pudding and put in oven long enough for meringue to brown.

— *Mary K. Breighner, Rudolph Breighner*

# Creamy Rice Pudding

*Makes 4 – 6 servings*

1 quart milk
1 cup rice
1 egg, well beaten
cinnamon

1 cup sugar
½ tsp. salt
½ tsp. vanilla

1. Cook rice in milk over double boiler until soft, about 1 – 1½ hours. Stir occasionally and add more milk if needed.

2. Remove 1 cup hot rice and milk from heat and gradually add to the egg. Then stir back into the rest of the hot rice and milk, along with the sugar, salt and vanilla.

3. Sprinkle with cinnamon and serve.

— *Lena King, Shreiner's Flowers*

# Strawberry Delight

*Makes 12 servings*

1 box Danish dessert
1 quart fresh strawberries
1 cup confectioner's sugar, heaping
2 Tbsp. milk
8-oz. pkg. cream cheese, softened
6 ozs. whipped topping
graham cracker crust

1. Use favorite recipe to make graham cracker crust. Spread in a 9″ × 13″ pan.

2. Follow package directions for making Danish dessert. Cool 10 minutes and fold in fresh strawberries. Set aside.

3. Beat sugar and milk together. Add softened cream cheese and beat again. Fold in whipped topping. Spread this mixture carefully over crust.

4. Spread strawberry and Danish mixture over cream cheese mixture. Refrigerate before serving.

All strawberry lovers will enjoy this!

— *Marilyn Denlinger, Irwin S. Widders Produce*

# Pineapple Delight

*Makes 8 – 10 servings*

| | |
|---|---|
| 2 3-oz. pkgs. orange gelatin | 1 pkg. mini-marshmallows |
| 3 oz. pkg. lemon gelatin | 1 container whipped topping |
| 10-oz. can chunk pineapple | 1 jar maraschino cherries |

1. In a bowl, mix orange gelatin according to instructions. In separate bowl, mix lemon gelatin according to instructions. Put into refrigerator until each one has set.
2. Drain pineapple and cherries. Cut gelatin into cubes. In a large bowl mix all ingredients.
3. Chill and serve.

*— Grace Evans, Shreiner's Flowers*

# Pineapple Dessert

*Makes 6 servings*

1 large pkg. vanilla pudding
1¾ cups pineapple juice
1 medium can crushed pineapple, undrained
4 apples, finely diced
miniature marshmallows (optional)

1. Follow directions on box of pudding. Substitute pineapple juice for water. Fold undrained pineapples and apples into this mixture.
2. Miniature marshmallows make a delicious and attractive addition.

*— Lois Thomas, C. H. Thomas and Son*

# Orange Fluff Dessert

*Makes 4 servings*

| | |
|---|---|
| 1 pkg. unflavored gelatin | 1 cup frozen orange juice |
| ¼ cup cold water | 2 egg whites |
| ½ cup boiling water | 1 cup fresh orange slices |

1. Mix gelatin in cold water. Add boiling water and stir until dissolved. Add undiluted frozen orange juice concentrate. Stir and chill until thickened.
2. Beat egg whites at high speed until frothy and fold into mixture. Beat mixture until frothy.
3. Decorate with fresh oranges and serve.

This fresh, fluffy dish is good for the diet-conscious—it has no sugar or egg yolks.

*— Mildred Brackbill, Utz's Potato Chips*

# Orange Custard Fondue

*Makes 3½ cups*

**3-oz. pkg. vanilla pudding**
**1¾ cups milk**
**2 cups whipped topping**
**2 Tbsp. orange juice**
**1 tsp. orange peel**
**Fresh Fruit Dippers: strawberries, pineapple chunks, cante-
loupe, honeydew, melon, pear, peach slices, apples, bananas, pound cake cubes**

1. Prepare pudding according to package directions using 1¾ cups milk. Cover with clear plastic and chill about 2 hours until thickened.
2. Beat pudding with rotary beater until smooth. Fold in whipped topping and orange juice. Top with orange peel.
3. Serve fondue with fresh fruit and cake cubes.
*— Ethel Stoner, John R. Stoner Vegetables*

# Blueberry Buckle

*Makes 9 – 12 servings*

*Batter Ingredients:*
**2 cups flour**
**¾ cup sugar**
**2½ tsp. baking powder**
**¾ tsp. salt**
**¼ cup shortening**
**¾ cup milk**
**1 egg**
**2 cups blueberries, well
drained**

*Topping Ingredients:*
**½ cup sugar**
**⅓ cup flour**
**½ tsp. cinnamon**
**¼ cup butter, softened**

1. Blend all batter ingredients except blueberries in blender for about half a minute. Carefully stir in blueberries. Spread mixture into a greased 9″-square pan.
2. Mix together all topping ingredients. Sprinkle over batter in pan. Bake at 375° for 45 – 50 minutes.
*— Marian Eisenberger, Spring Glen Farm Kitchens, Inc.*

◆

# Cheese Cake

*Makes 16 servings*

*Cheese Cake Ingredients:*

2 pkgs. unflavored gelatin
½ cup cold water
2 eggs
½ – ¾ cup sugar
¾ cup water
2 8-oz. pkgs. cream cheese, softened
12-oz. container whipped topping

*Graham Cracker Crust Ingredients:*

2 cups graham crackers, crushed
½ cup butter, melted
⅓ – ½ cup sugar

1. Mix all ingredients for the crust. Press firmly onto bottom of 9″ × 13″ baking dish. Bake at 350° about 5–8 minutes. Cool.
2. Dissolve gelatin in cold water. Set aside.
3. Over low heat mix egg yolks, sugar and water. Stir until mixed well and boiling. Let cool.
4. Beat egg whites until stiff.
5. Mix cream cheese with egg yolk mixture and gelatin. Fold in egg whites and whipped topping. Beat for a few minutes.
6. Pour cheese cake over graham cracker crust. Refrigerate several hours before serving.

— *Susie Beiler, Kauffman's Fruit Farm*

**Variation:**

1. Use ⅔ cup water and juice from ½ fresh lemon in egg yolk and sugar mixture.
2. Stir zest from 1 lemon (about 1 Tbsp.) into cream cheese, egg yolk and gelatin mixture.

I remember the women who used to pick strawberries for my father's stand on Central Market. They walked two miles from their homes to ours and started picking at 6 a.m. each morning during the two- to three-week strawberry season. They knew how to fill an "honest box" with big berries at the bottom as well as the top.

— **from the memories of the late Myrtle Howry Funk**

◆

# Oreo® Cookie Dessert

*Makes 12 – 14 servings*

1 large pkg. Oreo® cookies
8 Tbsp. butter, melted
2 pkgs. vanilla pudding
8-oz. pkg. cream cheese,
    softened

3½ cups milk
2 cups whipped topping

1. Crunch up cookies with a rolling pin. Pour melted butter over cookie crumbs. Press half of crumbs into the bottom of a 9″ × 13″ baking dish. Reserve remaining crumbs for topping.
2. Beat ½ cup milk with cream cheese until mixture is fluffy. Add pudding and remaining milk and mix well. Fold whipped topping into pudding mixture.
3. Spread pudding mixture over cookie crumbs. Spread reserved crumbs over pudding layer.
4. Chill and serve.

—*Donna Betancourt, Eisenberger's Baked Goods*

# Homemade Ice Cream

*Makes 4 quarts*

2 cups sugar
4 eggs
2 cups heavy cream
1 cup light cream

2 Tbsp. vanilla
½ tsp. salt
milk

1. Beat sugar and eggs together until light and thick (about 10 minutes). Add remaining ingredients, except milk, and mix well.
2. Pour into ice cream freezer can and add milk until can is about ⅔ full.
3. Layer ice and salt around the can in the freezer. Use crushed ice and do not skimp on salt.

This simple recipe yields delicious ice cream from start to finish in about an hour!

—*Joanne Warfel, S. Clyde Weaver, Inc.*

# Frozen Banana Split Dessert

*Makes 15 servings*

2 cups graham crackers,
    crushed
⅓ cup butter, melted
2 – 3 bananas
2 quarts ice cream
1 cup nuts, chopped
1 cup chocolate chips

½ cup butter
2 cups confectioner's sugar
1½ cups evaporated milk
1 tsp. vanilla
1 pint whipped cream
1 cup graham crackers,
    crushed

1. Prepare graham cracker crust by pouring ⅓ cup melted butter over 2 cups graham crackers. Mix well. Spoon this crust into bottom of 9″ × 13″ pan. Press down with spoon.
2. Slice bananas and lay over crust. Slice ice cream ½″ thick and lay on top of bananas. Sprinkle nuts over ice cream. Freeze till firm.
3. Melt chocolate chips and ½ cup butter over low heat. Add confectioner's sugar and evaporated milk to chocolate mixture. Cook until thickened, stirring constantly. Remove from heat and add vanilla. Cool slightly (not too long or it will become stiff). Pour over the ice cream. Freeze until ready to serve.
4. Before serving spread whipped cream over top. Sprinkle 1 cup graham cracker crumbs over all.

This cool refreshing dessert is great for special treats.
— *Joy Wadel, Irwin S. Widders Produce*

# Fruit Pizza

*Makes 8 servings*

*Filling Ingredients:*
8-oz. pkg. cream cheese,
    softened
½ cup sugar
8 ozs. whipped topping
1 tsp. lemon juice

*Glaze Ingredients:*
½ cup sugar
2 Tbsp. cornstarch
1 cup orange juice
¼ cup lemon juice

*Topping Ingredients:*
any variation of fresh or
    canned fruits

*Crust Ingredients:*
favorite sugar cookie recipe
    or Fruit Pizza crust recipe
    found on page 201

1. Mix ingredients for crust according to directions. Press into greased pizza pan and bake 10 – 20 minutes at 325° (until slightly brown).
2. Cream all ingredients for filling together and spread over cooled crust.

3. Arrange fruit over pizza as desired. Different colors make it more attractive.
4. Mix ingredients for glaze together and stir constantly over medium heat until thickened. Spoon over fruit while glaze is hot. (This glaze helps prevent fruit from turning brown.)
5. Cool pizza several hours before serving.

Attractive and very delicious!
— *Deb Warfel, S. Clyde Weaver, Inc.*

# Fruit Pizza Crust

*Makes crust for one pizza pan*

**2 cups flour**
**1 tsp. salt**
**⅔ cup shortening**
**3 – 4 Tbsp. ice water**
**⅔ cup sharp cheddar cheese, grated**

1. Mix together flour and salt. Cut in shortening.
2. Add ice water until mixture forms a ball. Work in the grated cheese with a fork or your fingers until well mixed. Press into greased pizza pan.
3. Bake dough 8 – 10 minutes at 475°. Prick throughout baking time with a fork.
— *Viv Hunt, Viv's Varieties*

# Kourabiedes

*Makes 4 dozen*

**1 lb. sweet butter**
**½ cup confectioner's sugar**
**2 lbs. flour (or little less)**

1. Cream butter about 20 minutes or until very fluffy. Add sugar and cream another 20 – 25 minutes. (You have to work for this!)
2. Sift flour. Add gradually to creamed mixture by hand. Do not use mixer. Work until dough is fluffy, never clumpy.
3. Grease hands. With a teaspoon, take a lump and roll in your hands. Form into oval, ball or any shape desired.
4. Place on greased cookie sheet and bake at 350° for 25 minutes. Let cool and dip into confectioner's sugar.
— *Koula Vakios, Koula's Greek Pastries*

# Diplos

*Makes about 35 diplos*

*Diplo Ingredients:*
1 cup milk
2 eggs, beaten
1 tsp. lemon juice
½ tsp. salt
1 cup plus 1 Tbsp. flour
1 tsp. sugar (optional)

*Syrup Ingredients:*
2 cups granulated sugar
1 cup water
1 – 1½ cups honey
2 – 3 whole cloves
1 cinnamon stick

*Other Ingredients:*
Diplo mold
enough oil for deep frying
1 cup walnuts, finely ground

1. Mix milk and eggs together. Add lemon juice. Stir in dry ingredients and mix until smooth. Batter should be runny.
2. Pour oil into deep frying pan. Heat until very hot. Place diplo mold into hot oil until it is hot. Carefully remove from oil and dip into batter. Do not immerse; rather, dip into batter about ¾ of way.
3. Place mold into hot oil. Batter will drop into oil. Fry until golden brown. Let cool on paper towels.
4. Mix all syrup ingredients. Cook until it thickens like honey. Let cool.
5. Drizzle syrup over diplos. Sprinkle with ground walnuts and serve.

—*Koula Vakios, Koula's Greek Pastries*

Koula Vakios sells this delicate pastry on Central Market. To make her diplos, she uses a mold which she received from her Greek mother-in-law at least 25 years ago.

# Finger Jello

*Makes 100 1″ squares*

4 pkgs. unflavored gelatin
3 3-oz. pkgs. fruit gelatin (cherry works well)
4 cups boiling water
2 cups dry (or uncreamed) cottage cheese

1. In a large bowl combine unflavored and flavored gelatins. Add boiling water and stir until gelatin dissolves. Add cottage cheese.
2. Pour into 9″ × 13″ baking pan and chill until firm. Cut into squares or various shapes with cookie cutters.

—*Mary Catherine Bowman, Shenk's Cheese Co.*

**Variation:**

Add fresh fruit. My daughter cuts bing cherries in half and adds them to the mixture.

# Chocolate Fudge

*Makes 60 pieces*

**3 6-oz. pkgs. semi-sweet chocolate chips**
**14-oz. can sweetened condensed milk**
**dash of salt**
**½ – 1 cup nuts, chopped**
**1½ tsp. vanilla**

1. In double boiler over medium heat melt chocolate chips with condensed milk. Remove from heat.
2. Stir in remaining ingredients. Spread evenly into a wax paper-lined 8″- or 9″-square pan.
3. Chill 2 hours or until firm. Turn fudge onto cutting board. Peel off paper and cut into squares. Store, loosely covered, in refrigerator.

Very creamy and rich!

*—Anna F. Kreider, Viv's Varieties*

**Variations:**
   1. Melt chocolate chips with condensed milk in microwave for 4 minutes on medium high.
   2. Use peanut butter chips instead of chocolate chips.
   3. Use mint chocolate chips instead of chocolate chips.

# Peanut Brittle Candy

**1 cup sugar**
**½ cup dark corn syrup**
**½ cup light corn syrup**
**1 Tbsp. water**

**2 cups raw peanuts**
**½ tsp. cinnamon**
**½ tsp. salt**
**¾ tsp. baking soda**

1. Mix sugar, dark and light corn syrup and water. Bring to a boil over medium heat. Boil for 2 minutes. Add peanuts and continue to boil until peanuts look like they are roasted brown.
2. Remove from heat. Add cinnamon, salt and baking soda and mix. Pour onto greased cookie sheet. Cool.
3. Break peanut brittle into pieces and store in a tight container.

*—Helen Thomas, Helen Thomas Produce*

◆

# Potato Butter Mints

*Makes 3 dozen mints*

¼ cup butter, softened
¼ cup warm mashed potatoes
1 lb. confectioner's sugar
any flavoring or coloring desired
small amount of granulated sugar

1. Cook potato. Mash, but do not add any milk, salt or butter.
2. Cream mashed potatoes and butter with mixer. Add confectioner's sugar slowly, eventually mixing with hands. Add a few drops of water or a little more confectioner's sugar—whichever is needed—to make dough workable.
3. Add flavoring or coloring, as desired. Mixture should be consistency of play dough.
4. Roll mint dough into balls or any shape desired. Roll each mint in granulated sugar.

—*Ruth Thomas, Helen Thomas Produce*

# CONDIMENTS

◆

# Concord Grape Butter

**4–6 cups Concord grapes**
**4–6 cups sugar**
**2 Tbsp. water**

1. Mix all ingredients and heat slowly until sugar dissolves.
2. When mixture comes to a full boil, boil for 20 minutes. Squeeze through food press and put into jars and seal.

Delicious spread for homemade bread!
— *Ruth Widders, Irwin S. Widders Produce*

# Apple Butter

*Makes 5 quarts*

**7 lbs. apples**
**3 lbs. brown sugar**
**1 cup vinegar or cider**
**2 Tbsp. powdered cinnamon**

1. Cook apples until soft. Press through a food press to make a sauce. This should yield about 16 cups of sauce.
2. Add brown sugar, vinegar and cinnamon to sauce and mix well.
3. Put into roast pan and bake at 350° for 3 hours, stirring several times.
4. Pour into jars and seal.

**Hint:** A mealy, cooking apple is best for this recipe.
— *Ruth Widders, Irwin S. Widders Produce*

# Long's Gourmet Seafood Sauce

*Makes 4–8 servings*

**4 ozs. chili sauce**
**1 oz. Long's horseradish**
**1 tsp. fresh lime juice**

**pinch Old Bay® seasoning**
**1 tsp. Worcestershire® sauce**
**4 drops Tabasco® sauce**

1. Mix all ingredients thoroughly.
2. Store in tightly covered jar in refrigerator.
— *Charles J. Long, Long's Horseradish*

# Long's Cocktail Sauce

*Makes 4 – 8 servings*

**2 cups ketchup**
**5-oz. jar Long's horseradish**
**1 Tbsp. Worcestershire®**
   **sauce**

**1 Tbsp. lemon juice**
**5 drops Tabasco® sauce**
**1 tsp. salt**

1. Mix all ingredients thoroughly.
2. Store inverted in a tightly covered jar in refrigerator.

Cocktail sauce is a favorite for shrimp, but it is also delicious on hot dogs, hamburgers and other seafood.

*— Charles J. Long, Long's Horseradish*

**Variations:**
   1. Delete salt for no-salt diets.
   2. If sauce is too hot, add more ketchup to make it milder.
   3. If sauce is too thick, add equal parts water and vinegar to thin.

# Hot Bacon Dressing

*Makes 8 – 10 servings*

**½ lb. bacon**
**1 cup sugar**
**½ – 1 cup vinegar, to desired**
   **taste**
**1 cup water**

**1 egg beaten**
**3 Tbsp. flour**
**½ tsp. mustard**

1. Cook bacon until crisp. Drain well. Crumble.
2. Mix all ingredients except bacon over medium heat in a sauce-pan. Heat to a low boil. Reduce to low heat and cook until dressing has thickened.
3. Add crushed bacon and serve over shredded lettuce.

**Hint:** Mixture will boil over if not watched.

*— Debbie Buhay, Shenk's Cheese Co.*

# Blue Cheese Dip or Dressing

*Makes 8 servings*

| | |
|---|---|
| 1 lb. blue cheese | ½ cup parsley, chopped |
| 2 cups sour cream | ¼ cup capers, drained |
| 1 small onion, chopped | salt and pepper to taste |

1. Blend half of blue cheese with all other ingredients. Crumble remaining blue cheese into mixture and mix gently by hand.
2. If using as a dip, garnish with extra parsley.
3. If using as a dressing, thin to desired consistency with milk or cream.

*—Sam Neff, S. Clyde Weaver, Inc.*

**Variation:**
Add bit of dry mustard or garlic powder.

# Carrot Dip

| | |
|---|---|
| 8 oz. pkg. cream cheese, softened | 1 pkg. George Washington's® seasoning and broth mix |
| 1 Tbsp. milk | 1 tsp. chives, chopped |
| 1 Tbsp. mayonnaise | 1 small onion, grated |
| 1 Tbsp. sour cream | 1 carrot, grated |

1. Cream softened cream cheese. Add milk, mayonnaise, sour cream, seasoning and chives.
2. Stir in onions and carrots and mix well.
3. Serve with a variety of fresh, raw vegetables.

*—Ethel Stoner, John R. Stoner Vegetables*

**Variation:**
Substitute onion soup mix for George Washington's® seasoning.

From the beginning of our business, women have been central to the success of S. Clyde Weaver. My grandparents bought the stand around 1930 and Grandmother Emma ran the business. In those days, tending market was one of the few acceptable outside-the-home jobs for women. My mother and aunt were very important during the second generation when the business was owned by my father and uncle. Today women still play a central role in our business.

*—Sam Neff, S. Clyde Weaver, Inc.*

# Vegetable Dip

*Makes 1 pint*

**8-oz. pkg. cream cheese, softened**
**2 pkgs. George Washington's® seasoning and broth mix**
**⅔ cup or less sour cream**

1. Blend cream cheese and seasoning and mix well.
2. Add sour cream and mix well.
3. Chill overnight and serve with raw vegetables.
—*Joyce Deiter, Eisenberger's Baked Goods*

**Variation:**
Substitute your own favorite soup mix for George Washington's® seasoning and broth mix.

# Chipped Beef Spread

*Makes 2–3 cups*

**16 ozs. cream cheese, softened**
**8 ozs. schmierkase**
**8 ozs. dried beef, chopped**
**1 small green pepper, chopped**
**1 small onion, chopped**
**¼ cup English walnuts, chopped**
**½–1 tsp. seasoned salt**

1. Put all ingredients into blender or food processor and mix well.
2. Refrigerate overnight.
3. Serve with assorted crackers and fresh vegetables.
—*Debbie Buhay, Shenk's Cheese Co.*

**Variation:**
Substitute sour cream for schmierkase.

# Cream Topping for Fresh Fruit

*Makes 3 cups topping*

**1 cup vanilla ice cream**
**½ cup sour cream**
**¼ cup sugar**
**1 tsp. vanilla**
**1 cup whipped topping**

1. Combine all ingredients.
2. Serve with fruit and angel food cake.
—*Ethel Stoner, John R. Stoner Vegetables*

◆

# Fruit Dip for Fresh Fruit

**8-oz. pkg. cream cheese, softened**
**7-oz. jar marshmallow cream**
**6 Tbsp. orange or lemon juice**

1. Blend all ingredients for dip together. Mix until smooth.
2. Serve on tray with fruit (apples, strawberries, melon balls, grapes, kiwi slices, pineapple chunks, etc.). Colored toothpicks help make this party food more attractive.

Simple, yet favorite, tray for a party. May also be served on top of molded fruit jello.

*—Marilyn Denlinger, Irwin S. Widders Produce*

# Egg Cheese

*Makes 6 servings*

**2 cups sweet milk**
**1 Tbsp. flour**
**1 Tbsp. sugar**
**3 eggs**
**1 cup buttermilk**

1. Heat sweet milk almost to scalding.
2. Mix flour, sugar, eggs and buttermilk and add to hot milk. Stir until it almost reaches a boil.
3. Let boil slowly for 15 minutes until mixture separates and has yellow color on top.
4. Drain and strain in an egg cheese mold or strainer until cold.
5. Unmold onto plate and serve with King Syrup® or light molasses.

This old-fashioned recipe was a favorite of Ted Shenk's mother. Different, but good!

*—Doris Shenk, Donegal Gardens*

# Homemade Yogurt

*Makes 1 quart*

**1 scant quart milk**
**⅓ cup non-instant dry milk**
**1 Tbsp. plain yogurt**

1. Bring scant quart milk to almost boiling point (forms thin layer on top).
2. Cool until comfortable to your little finger. Add dry milk and mix thoroughly. Add plain yogurt and mix well again.
3. Pour mixture into quart jar and place in large cooking kettle with warm water (comfortable to your hand). Cover kettle and put into unlighted oven or other warm place. Let set for 3 hours or until yogurt has set.

**Hint:** To make new yogurt, one must always add a starter from a previous making or buy fresh plain yogurt from a store.
*—Fannie S. Fisher, Tom's Flower Garden*

**Variation:**
Stir in your favorite jelly or fruit. Refrigerate and enjoy!

# Vanilla Extract

*Makes 1 cup*

**1 vanilla bean (Tahitian, preferred)**
**1 cup vodka (unflavored rum, brandy or grain alcohol will also do)**

1. Take kitchen scissors and cut vanilla bean in half to expose seeds.
2. Put alcohol into bottle with cap. Add split vanilla bean and shake.
3. Let sit for at least 2 months before using. The longer it sits the better it will be.

This vanilla extract is pure. Vanilla extracts purchased at supermarkets contain water, alcohol, corn syrup, caramel coloring and often only a small amount of vanilla bean.
*—Brad Loercher, Parsley Porch*

# Recipe for Living

**2 heaping cups patience**
**1 heartful of love**
**1 handful of understanding**
**1 dash of laughter**
**1 bunch of fresh flowers**

1. Mix all ingredients. Sprinkle generously with kindness.
2. Add plenty of faith.

Give fresh flowers with joy and brighten someone's day!

— *Viv Hunt, Viv's Varieties*

# Flowers

Flowers enhance many foods. Use as a garnish instead of parsley, watercress or curly greens.

We have been selling flowers on the market stand for 50 years this year.

— *Edith R. Weaver, Frank Weaver Greenhouses*

> **Billy and Pauly have been a fixture at Central Market for as long as I can remember. They live in a group home in Lancaster and come in at 4 a.m. to help standholders unload their purchases. Pauly cannot talk but everyone on market knows how to communicate with him. He used to always help Angie Collata carry her fresh fruit to her stand.**
> — *Viv Hunt, Viv's Varieties*

# Central Market Standholders

Note: If it was known that a stand was purchased at a December auction, it was given a founding date in the next year. Some information was obtained directly from the standholders, some came from newspaper articles, and some came from the few available official records.

**B-7,8  Bagels and More**
(since 1981)
Bagels and other baked goods

**H-16  The Baker's Basket**
(since 1988)
Baked goods

**E-13,14,15,16  Baltozer's Candies**
(since 1982)
Candy

**F-8,9,10,11  Amos Barr Produce**
(since c. 1965)
Fruits, vegetables

**F-12, G-7,8  James Barr Produce**
(since 1975)
Fruits, vegetables

**E-9,10  Baskets of Central Market**
(since 1988)
Baskets

**E-7,8  Andrew E. Beiler**
(since 1986)
Crafts, gifts

**M-1,2,3,4  Mr. Bill's Seafood**
(since 1989)
Seafood

**D-17,18  Bird-in-Hand Restaurant Bakery**
(since 1985)
Baked goods

**C-18  Bitners**
(since c. 1920s)
Vegetables and poultry

**A-6,7  James Boas**
(since 1985)
Puerto Rican fruits and vegetables

**D-13,14  Rudolph Breighner**
(since c. 1880s)
Fruit, vegetables, poultry, eggs

**G-9,10  Brenneman Farm**
(since c. 1974)
Fruit, vegetables, plants, baked goods

**G-17,18,19  Donegal Gardens**
(since 1858 or before)
Fruit and vegetables

H-17,18  **Dutch Haven Bake Shop**
(since 1981)
Baked goods

J-3,4  **Eisenberger's Baked Goods**
(since c. 1939)
Baked goods

B-3,4,5,6  **Enck's**
(since 1927)
Smoked meats and cheeses

D-9,10,11,12  **Funk Brothers, Inc.**
(since c. 1910 or before)
Vegetables, fruits, turkeys

K-14,15  **German Deli**
(since 1978)
Meat, cheese, German specialties

J-1,2  **Givant's Bakery**
(since 1959)
Baked goods

A-4,5 H-3,4  **The Goodie Shoppe**
(since 1981)
Baked goods, salads

E-17,18,19  **Rohrer M. Groff**
(since c. 1964)
Vegetables

M-10  **Habibi's**
(since 1989)
Middle-Eastern baked goods

J-17,18  **Charles Hess**
(since c. 1880s)
Baked goods, vegetables, eggs

H-19, J-19  **Hidden Acres Flowers**
(since 1978)
Flowers, plants

D-15,16  **Hodecker's**
(since c. 1920s or before)
Celery

A-8,9,10  **Horn of Plenty**
(since 1981)
Fruits and vegetables

K-1,2,3,4  **Robert P. Howry, Inc.**
(since 1931)
Fresh meat

E-1,2,3,4  **Kauffman's Fruit Farms**
(since c. 1939)
Fruit, eggs, spreads, bulk food

A-1,2,3  **Kiefer's Meats and Cheese**
(since c. 1940s)
Smoked meats, cheese, salads

L-9,10  **Kim's Candies**
(since 1986)
Candy, egg rolls

F-1  **Koula's Greek Pastries**
(since 1979)
Greek pastries

J-11,12  **Kreider's**
(since 1963)
Celery

F-13,14,15,16  **Sallie Y. Lapp**
(since 1980)
Crafts, snacks, pretzels

H-10  **Long's Horseradish**
(since 1939)
Horseradish, relishes

M-6,7,8,9  **Marion Cheese**
(since 1985)
Cheese, salads, gourmet food

C-9,10  **Martin's**
(since 1984)
Cheese, salads, desserts, relishes

J-15,16  **Martin's Home Baked Goods**
(since 1985)
Baked goods, eggs, noodles, chow chow

C-5,6,7,8  **C.Z. Martin Sons**
(since 1923)
Smoked meats and cheese

K-9,10,11  **John M. Markley Meats**
(since 1881)
Beef, veal, pork, lamb

A-11  **Maurer's Sauce Spot**
(since 1976)
Sauce, mustard, jam, jelly, dressings

H-15  **McComsey Family**
(since c. 1950)
Crafts, dolls

G-11,12  **Robert S. Meck**
(since 1974)
Fruit and vegetables

E-5,6  **Michael's Homestyle Breads**
(since 1988)
Breads and other baked goods

M-5  **Melissa's Favorites**
(since 1979)
Nuts, dried fruits, snacks

F-2,3,4  **Mumma's Pretzel Bakery**
(since 1986)
Pretzels and snacks

F-18,19  **Nancy's Goodies**
(since 1938)
Baked goods

A-12,13,14  **New Holland Seafood**
(since c. 1971)
Seafood

F-7  **Ruth Nolt**
(since 1964)
Flowers

B-1,2  **Nye's Sandwich Haus**
(since 1980)
Sandwiches, soft drinks

J-13,14  **Caroline Pannel**
(since 1974)
Fruits and vegetables

H-5,6  **Pennsylvania Dutch Gifts**
(since 1984)
Gifts

D-19  **Parsley Porch**
(since 1985)
Spices and herbs

K-16,17  **Peter Raub**
(since 1989)
Gourmet food

K-5,6,7  **Paul L. Sensenig and Sons**
(since 1981)
Smoked meat and cheese

D-5,6,7,8  **Shenk's Cheese Co.**
(since 1880s)
Cup cheese, ball cheese, spreads

D-1,2,3,4  **Shreiner's Flowers**
(since c. 1930)
Flowers

F-17  **Shutt's Candy**
(since 1966)
Candy

K-12,13  **Slaymaker's**
(since 1976)
Poultry and eggs

L-1,2,3  **The Spice Stand**
(since 1977)
Coffee beans, tea, spices, snacks

C-14,15,16,17  **Spring Glen Farm Kitchens, Inc.**
(since 1966)
Salads, desserts, spreads

G-13,14,15,16  **John R. Stoner
Vegetables**
(since c. 1900)
Fruit and vegetables

C-1,2,3,4  **C.H. Thomas and Son**
(since 1913)
Fresh beef and pork

C-19,20  **Helen Thomas Produce**
(since 1931)
Fruit and vegetables

G-3,4,5,6  **Tom's Flower Garden**
(since 1984)
Flowers

L-7,8  **Utz's Potato Chips**
(since c. 1925)
Potato chips and snacks

G-1,2  **Vie d'Or**
(since 1986)
Baked goods

J-5,6  **Viv's Varieties**
(since c. 1880s)
Crafts, flowers

E-11,12  **Haines T. Walker**
(since 1986)
Fruits and vegetables

B-15,16,17  **D.M. Weaver and Sons, Inc.**
(since 1911)
Smoked meat, cheeses

J-7,8,9,10  **Frank Weaver Greenhouses**
(since c. 1939)
Fresh and dried flowers, plants

K-8, L-4,5,6  **S. Clyde Weaver, Inc.**
(since c. 1929)
Smoked meat and cheese

H-11,12,13,14  **Irwin S. Widders Produce**
(since 1964)
Fruit and vegetables

B-9,10,11,12,13,14  **Willow Valley Farm**
(since 1945)
Baked goods, poultry, barbecued chicken

F-5,6  **Windows on Steinman Park**
(since 1986)
Baked goods

H-7,8,9  **The Wooden Carrousel**
(since 1986)
Crafts, candy

# Central Market Cookbook Index

# Bibliography

Baer, Meryl. *The Central Market: A Colonial Legacy.* Masters Dissertation, Pennsylvania State University Graduate School, 1975.

Ducker, Dan. "History of Lancaster's Central Market," *Susquehanna,* Vol. 8, No. 11 (November 1983), 19–25.

Heisey, M. Luther. *The Famed Markets of Lancaster, Pa.* n.p.: M. Luther Heisey, 1949.

McGee, Nancy. "Central Market, Let's Look Inside," *Lancaster County,* Vol. 3, No. 2 (July/August 1989), 24–27.

Rohrer, Kay. "Lancaster History in its Markets," *Lancaster Sunday News* (May 25, 1986).

Thomas, Martha. "They Have a Good Market in This Town," *Early American Life* (August 1978), 49, 50.

# About the Authors

Phyllis Pellman Good is a native of Lancaster County, Pennsylvania. As a teenager she worked on Central Market, and today, as a resident of Lancaster City, shops there. She edits books related to the Amish and Mennonites, as well as **Festival Quarterly,** a magazine exploring the arts, faith and culture of Mennonite peoples.

Good is the author of **Cooking and Memories, The Festival Cookbook: Four Seasons of Favorites,** and **The Best of Amish Cooking.** She is co-author of **From Amish and Mennonite Kitchens** with Rachel Thomas Pellman and of **20 Most Asked Questions About the Amish and Mennonites,** written with her husband, Merle.

The Goods live in Lancaster, Pa., and are the parents of two daughters.

Louise Stoltzfus is also a native of Lancaster County, Pennsylvania. She is Assistant Director of The People's Place Gallery, Assistant Manager of The Old Road Furniture Company, both in Intercourse, Pennsylvania, and works parttime with Good Books.

After having lived in Sarasota, Florida, for six years, she recently returned to Lancaster. She lives on a wooded ridge near Paradise, Pennsylvania.